Military Governance in Pakistan

Other Books From the Same Author

1. India's National Security
2. A Quest For Happiness (Spiritual)
3. A Man Who Saw God (Fiction)

Military Governance In Pakistan

Brig. R.A. Singh VSM (Retd.)

Raj Publications

New Delhi - 110002

Military Governance in Pakistan

2019

₹ 495

ISBN 978-81-86208-57-1

Published by : **Raj Publications**

108, 4855/24, Ansari Road,
Daryaganj, New Delhi - 110002
Tel. : 011-23250939, 09811010939
E-mail: rajpublications@yahoo.co.in

Laser Typesetting : Aarti Computers, Delhi

Printed at : Balaji Offset, Delhi

PRINTED IN INDIA

Dedicated to

My father Late Shri Nar Singh Ji,
who always treated me as a young boy
even when I had become a flag officer
in the Indian Army

PREFACE

Pakistan politics is a bizarre alternation between military rulers and civilian government. The army in Pak has played and continues to play a vital role in shaping of the country since 1947. Though Pak was founded as a democratic country after partition, but did not last for long due to corrupt Chaotic and anarchic rule of the feudal and capitalist' politicians, who could not even formulate a proper constitution for their country. The army in Pak has remained as one of the most powerful institutions and has on number of occasions overthrown democratically elected governments on the basis of mismanagement and corruption. Even whenever there was a civilian government in power, it was an unwritten code of conduct that the Army in Pak was consulted before taking important decision or formulating a policy, particularly if it concerned India. The political leadership in Pak is aware that military leaders can step into political arena at will, even if the situation does not warrant so.

Pakistan received aid from US between 1954 and 1965, which tremendously augmented their defence capabilities. New arms and equipment were purchased, military bases were expanded and a few new ones were created including large number of new raisings and two corps Headquaters'. US also helped Pak troop in imparting training to them and in turn Pak allowed US to establish bases within Pak border to Spy on Soviet Union. Pak also developed close military ties with many middle eastern countries, particularly during FM Ayub Khan's regime.

The relations with India have always been bitter. They have always provided military support to separatists in Kashmir and now has been sponsoring terrorism in India from across the border, with well identified training camps in POK. They also helped Sikh movement in Indian Punjab during General Zia ul Haq' rule to distablize India. In addition to fighting wars with India, it tried a few tactical tricks in Siachen and Kargil sectors, in both the places it had to cut a sorry figure. After 9/11, the Pak army is engaged in protracted low intensity operations along its western borders in Afganistan, against Taliban, in support of US led forces. The intensity of Pak sponsored terrorism in India has not yet diminished.

Pak today, is governed by a military ruler. The military has gained strength by opportunistically aliging itself with US, China and Saudi Arabia. The military in Pak has ruled for a number of years in its history and has cultivated relations with the fundamentalist islamic clergy to strengthen its hold on power.

Infact military is a bastion of islamists who are influenced by fundamentalist movements. Pak army has been a key source of instability in the region, internally it has distablized number of properly elected popular governments. They have been the main supporters of Taliban throughout. ISI of Pak is believed to have fathered Taliban. This intelligence agancy is reported to have been deeply involved in heroin smuggling operations. After 9/11 attacks in US, Pak has joined US led forces in war on terror against Taliban in Afganistan, though its has earned a dubious reputation. Pak has deployed almost 72,000 troops along the border with Afganistan.

In islamisation, it contributed to the growth of religious extremism. Madrasas sprung up all over the country, originally conceived as a welfare set up, but many have gone out of control. During General Zia ul Haq's time, funds for these madrasas came from Saudi Arabia and Gulf states. The madrasas preach terrorism by perverting the faith.

It is now well established fact that islamic terrorism has its links with Pak, whether it is Al Qaida, Taliban, Laskar-e-Toiba or Jaise Mohammad. Terrorist plots from September 11 attacks to Madrid, to London, to Mumbai, have roots in Islamabad. In addition to breeding and aiding terrorism, Pak has also supplied nuclear technology to Iran and North Korea. Imagine a country that is ruled by a military ruler, has plenty of nuclear technology and bombs and is known to harbour vicious international terrorists; needs to be pressurised by all but unfortunately it is a prime ally of US today in war on terror. 'Pak' level of corruption and lack of accountability of its institutions provide a perfect breeding ground for the terrorists. The entire game plan has already gone out of its military leaders hands and now one has to wait and see the fate of many, involved in this dirty game.

Seeing the happenings in Pak and in the region, I as an ex-armyman could not resist a deep look into the events and this book is the result of that curiosity. The events have been covered with effect from 1947 to give a complete profile, how a newly independent state messed up its political events. The contribution has come from various sources, from defence library, war vaterns, military correspondents, newspapers and magazines. This covers the policies and attitudes of various military leaders which led to swift take over, one after another and also the lessons to be drawn from it. The data has been checked and compared with the existing records for its correctness. Any human error is requested to be overlooked.

I have abstained from passing any opinion or judgement on various events unless it were absolutely inescapable to complete the text. The narrative itself projects the story and future courses of action and I feel there is no need to sway the readers to one side or the other.

I shall be failing, if I do not mention about my wife 'Rama' who has always been a source of inspiration for me and has indirectly contributed a lot in production of this book, without which, I would have probably taken years to complete the job.

Brig. R.A. Singh
VSM (Retd.)

Contents

1

Military Elites in National Politics

The role of military elites in the political development of the emerging countries of the world has become a subject of serious and sustained concern. Throughout the first decade of post world war II era, it was generally assuemed that the future of the newly independent states lay in the hands of their politicians, bureaucrats or their intellectuals. During the late fifties and early sixties, however it became apparent that the military elites were playing an increasingly larger part in the domestic affairs of many of the emerging states.

The military leaders are by origin, sensitive to the feelings of the rural population. Thus they feel free to support, destroy or replace the civilian leadership as they see fit. Those who participated in struggle for independence movements also look upon themselves as the guardian of the territorial integrity of the nation. They were among the first to acquire organisational skills and technological capabilities. The military leaders are usually short of patience and are unwilling to tolerate political and social chaos. They always feel that more can be achieved by discipline and regimentation. They feel that the politicians are corrupt and deceptive. The military leaders feel obliged to take over when politicians fail to provide efficient and popular governance.

The newly independent states have to maintain a large standing military forces to meet the internal and external threats. The military force participate in variety of national activities of a new state. They thus contribute indirectly and in varying degrees to political development through conduct of civic action programs in the field of education, training, public works, agriculture, transport, communication, health and sanitation.

Over a period as the threats to national security persisted or even increased, the military elites became conspicous segments of the society in some of the newly independent states. In number of such states, of course except India, they developed a significant potential as a political force. The potential has been realized by intervention in domestic politics at the highest level. In so doing, the military elites assumed the role of constitutional caretaker or reformers. While playing the role of constitutional caretaker, the military leaders seize the reign of power, ostensibly to establish conditions under which political authority may be eventually returned to the civilian government through constitutional procedures.

In many new states, military coup succeeded because people rarely questioned the legitimacy of the take over, nor did they understand the super imposed, post independence political leadership. Besides, political instability, pessimism and economic failure simply encouraged the populace to accept austere descipline and a fresh change and a non-political military leaders were the heros and were usually popular with the masses. The military regime acted swiftly and sometimes offered pragmatic concessions such as an early return to a constitutional system and restoration of political parties. But only very late did they realize the need for creating their own circle of influence. It is therefore amply clear that in small developing countries, the strict descipline and political stability of military rule are preferred by the people to the inefficiency and instability of a democratic government. In short the military coup d'etat may therefore be regarded as providing necessary and tolerable periods of transition. As the state becomes modernised and differentiated, military leaders will no longer be able to take over the government and operate it directly. As a general rule countries create a reliable military profession that usually can not rule directly.

Some of the important reasons for Military take over in the newly independent states are:-

(a) During the years since the end of world war II, large military forces have been establish, trained, equipped and deployed to deter or to fight aggression. As threats to national security have continued, the prestige of the military man has risen and with it the political potential of the military elite.

(b) The armed forces contributed directly and in varying degrees to political development through the conduct of military civic action programs.

(c) Intervention in domestic politics by the military man is attributed primarily to the failure of the civilians political leadership to cope with internal and external problems — and lack of cohesion within and between the civil elites. In each case, the military elite was the only organisation and disciplined group capable of creating those conditions of order and stability which could lead to political, social and economic progress. The military take over then mostly gets legitimatised through constitutional process.

Major Military Interventions — World Over

Africa

Military motivation for interventions in politics in Africa have been similar to motivations elsewhere. A few coups have been radical, seeking extensive social, economic or political change. Some have been little conservative trying to stablize the existing system by imposing political order or by carrying out procedural reforms to make the government more efficient. Several have sought primarily a change in ruling personnel without significant changes in the style or the context of the government. Several times, sectional or tribal concerns have induced military man to intervene. More common in sub Saharan Africa than elsewhere, has been political involvement aimed at satisfying material grievances held collectively by the the military forces pay, prerequisites, promotions and administrative matters.

The armed forces in Sub Saharan Africa are multi functional. They assume or are given internal security and civic duties in addition to strategic ones, as part of national policy. African armies have been involved in domestic policies since independence. Calandestine military involvement in politics was common in the post war period in the old independent African states, Liberia and Ethopia. The first state to get its independence in 1950s, Sudan also was the first to be governed by its military forces. Between 1958 and 1965 there were a number of interventions including attempted coups, assassinations or mutinies by military personnel but most of those were quickly suppressed. In several countries the military leaders acted on a veto group blocking policies which threatened their positions and they sometimes made or influenced broder policies.

The strength of armed forces of these states is very small and a very small part of national budged is spent on defence. This is particularly so since African resources are severely limited. In nations where modern skills are scarce, military civic action programs are aften advocated as a means to make use of the technical training and man power of the armed forces in the national development effort. But it has also been seen that military leader's zeal for modernisation only illustrates a passion for control. Also the association of military forces with development has not been primarily a practical employment of scarce resources but rather has been an effort to establish norms for national evolution.

The use of military forces in internal security tasks serves the political function of maintaining the strength and stability of the regime by suppressing domestic opponents. In these states troops have been used at least once to put down labour strikes, political dissensions or other manifested discontents. One obivious' variable affecting the importance of the military forces security function is the extent to which other state security agencies effectively maintain order. In most of these states military forces have been employed continuously as instruments of national foreign policy. Thus far there has been little troop movements across national borders except minor border violations and threatening troops manouvres within national borders. The military forces symbolic role in development has proved to be far more significant than the organisational role.

Most African coups generally have been attributed to the progressive disintegration of civilian politician's ability and the will to rule. Civilian leaders are said to have failed to act relevantly and thus military men were obliged to intervene. In this view, interventions have resulted from reactive rather than designed militarism.

Asia

Since the end of Second World War the international tensions created by communist belligerence and by the prolonged dispute between India and Pakistan have resulted in the establishment of large standing armies in South Korea, South Vietnam, Thailand, Pakistan and India. As the threat to national security increased, the military elites became more powerful and important segment of the society. Some of the major interventions in the countries of Asia are discussed as under:-

(a) **Thailand**. Thailand military elites played a dominant role in politics since 1932 when a group of army officers brought an end to the absolute monarchy and established a constitutional government. Subsequently the military officers became either the caretakers or behind the scene supporters of the civil regime in power, Switching from the supporter to caretakers role as deemed necessary the main reason for military intervention was lack of a viable political alternative.

(b) **South Vietnam**. In South Vietnam, unlike Thailand, the military leaders lately began to play a decisive role in domestic politics. In Nov 1963, army coup to overthrow President Ngo-dinh-Diem, the military constituted the only element in a complex and conflicting, ethnic, religious, political and economic interest, that was sufficiently strong reason for them to depose his authoritarian regime.

(c) **South Korea**. The military elites seized control of the country in 1961. There was civilian disorder in the county. Military leaders overthrew John M. Chang, the prime minister and the steps were taken to restore public order, to reduce corruption and initiate a program to stimulate economic growth.

(d) **Burma**. In Burma (Myanmar) civilian government failed to solve the problems of nation building which included mainly shortage of capital, absence of trained personnel, inadequate social and educational facilities, excessive population in relation to land and grossly inadequate and imprefect means to mobalize both material and human resources. The other problem was the conflict between urban and rural areas and communist insurrection and revolt by ethnic minorities during 12 years of civilian control. The military coup of 02 May 1962 was due to U.Nu, the PM's inability to reconcile conflict among his followers. The main reasons cited for his downfall, were adoption of Buddhism as a state religion and promise of statehood for the Arakanese and the Mons at the expense of national unity.

(e) **Pakistan.** The military leaders assume power to sweep away all vestiges of the old order and to create a new political institution. In 1958, Pak was beset by a myriad of problems which had accumulated when official failed to provide for the progressive social, economic and political development of the country. The military elite considered the situation serious enough to warrant its intervention. General Ayub Khan declared martial law and proceeded systematically to restructure the existing political mechanism. Pak was introduced to the concept of basic democracy based on the election of the representative for every 1000 to 1500 people. In accordance with the provisions of a new constitution promulgated in 1962, a presidential election was held in 1965 with General Ayub Khan emerging victorious. There after military leaders kept intervening at will in Pak. Pak has been ruled by the military leaders for a large portion of time since its independence in 1947. The armed forces are highly respected in the civil society and is a top institution in the country. 06 September is known as 'Defence Day' to commemorate the military role in nation building in Pak.

Apolitical Elite of India

The military leaders in India have remained essential outside the political arena for three major reasons. First, the Indian political system and leadership has been relatively effective in discharging its constitutional responsibilities. Second, Indian federalism presents an almost insurmountable obstacle to any seizure of power by the military forces. The chief ministers of States of Indian federation are capable of putting up resistance and defeating all military ill designs. Finally the military professional in India were down graded administratively and socially during long era of non-alignment which followed India's independence, Infact at one stage the politician felt that the expenditure on maintaining a large standing military force was a sheer waste and undue burden on the economy of India. It was only when the Chinese attacked India in 1962 and the country was humiliated due to its ill prepared and neglected army, that a rethink to revitalize the military force began.

In any case if India had also suffered from military laws and military dictatorship on the pattern of Pak, it would have been in three to four separate segments by this day. India is most heterogenous than Pak but India has been kept in one piece by the noise and Chaos of its democracy.

2

THE PARTITION OF INDIA — 1947

Till as late as 1946, the Muslim League was prepared to accept autonomy. But their price for the unity was based on undemocratic and unacceptable demands. They wanted reserved seats for muslims much more than their population and Mr. Jinnah was to be the prime minister. The Congress had promised several constitutional protections for muslims to practise their religion and muslims to have their own legislation in matters of personal law and personal property. But Muslim League rejected the proposal and insisted on the partition as the only solution. The muslim had connived with British to present 'Partition' as a fait accompli. Though muslim elites were against partition, but with great regret many accepted it as a temporary setback, but felt that once the Britishers left, the future would be different.

Muslim League and the British were taking no chances. To ensure that Hindus and Muslims did not get together to reverse the decision, the muslim league with the British backing resorted to several acts of backmail and terror against Pak's Hindus and Sikh minorities. Arson, rape and mass murder resulted in an unprecedented exodus of millions refugees, with its inevitable anti muslim blacklash in India. Five millions Hindus and Sikhs and seven millions muslims migrated to India and Pak respectively and over a million people died in the process.

The murderous episode errupted from the peculiar alchemy of the sub continent. It sprang first from the inflamable nature of the people and their beliefs. Religious hatred had been nurtured through generations, of economic, social and political rivalries between the communities and manipulated continually by ignorant or unscrupulous leaders.

The British Parliament by an act on 18 July 1947, created two dominions ie India and Pak and provided for complete end of British control over India with effect from 15 Aug. 1947.

The British government devided the British India between India and Pak. The division of British Indian Army occured in which Pak received Six Armoured, eight Artillery and eight Infantry regiments compared to forty Armoured, forty Artillery and twenty one Infantry regiments went to India. The partition council which was chaired by the Viceroy of India, Lord Mountbatten, the leaders of Indian National Congress and Muslim League had agreed that the British Indian Army of 11,800 officers and 500,000 enlisted personnel, be divided to the ratio of 64% for India and 36% to Pak. By 15 Aug 1947, both the countries had full control over their armed forces.

Jammu & Kashmir Operations - 1947-48

Jammu & Kashmir (J&K) had common border with India and Pak at the time of partition in 1947. Maharaja Hari Singh was still undecided as to which side to join, either India or Pak. Pak having sensed the vulnerability of the situation, launched an attack on Kashmir. Thousands of tribals who are expert in plunder and looting were collected at Rawalpindi (Pak) and were issued with arms and ammunition. The State force of J&K that time consisted of only nine infantry battalions with Headquarters at Srinagar (J&K), but troops were spread all over ie. Jammu, Punch and Jhangar (all in J&K), that too in small sub units which could not be easily collected. In anycase this State force was not capable of meeting such an aggression. They were basically meant to carryout garrison duties and render aid to civil authorities when needed.

The Pak army based its operational plan on the above premise and weakness of the State forces, thinking to grab local towns around Srinagar immediately and then capture Srinagar, the State Capital. Pakistan also carried out communal propaganda just to provoke the feeling of the masses and particularly the troops of the state force who were predominantly muslims. Though it did not affect the civil population but some men of the state force did desert with weapons and helped the aggressor, in terms of guidance, intelligence etc. The main highway into Kashmir, the road Murree-Kohala-Damel-Srinagar which then passed through Pak was used by the aggressors. The main Pak column advanced on the road to reach Srinagar and plan was to block the entry at Banihal Pass from Indian side. Capture of Srinagar airfield also formed part of the plan. The column consisted of approximately 5000 troops. They used civilian trucks and lorries to travel.

There was just a battalion of State force to stop them on this axis. With little resistance the invaders reached the next very day at Garhi, Chinnari and Chakothi. However J&K State force managed to blow a girder bridge at Uri nallah which delayed the advance of the Pak column by four days. After that Baramulla which in 34 miles from the border fell to the invader without much resistance, on 28 Oct 1947. Before that Mahura power house was also damaged on 24 Oct 47, which cut off the electricity in Srinagar and around. The invaders looted Baramulla, plundered and raped women. Some of them returned to Pak with women and wealth. This resulted delay in their advance to Srinagar and thus it was saved from falling to invaders.

On 26 Oct 47 Maharaja Hari Singh signed an accession instrument in favour of India. India immediately then moved troops to Baramulla and

Srinagar to restore the situation and protect Srinagar airfield from falling to the invaders. Most of the troops were moved by air. *Uri* was recaptured on 13 Nov. 1947.

Pak also moved Laskars and regular troops from Sialkot to Jammu. Bhimber fell on 28 October 47 and Bagh was burnt by Pakistanis. Large number of civilians were killed by the invaders in the area of Rawalkot. In view of the gravity of situation, reinforcement were sent by India to this sector. Not going into the details of each battle that ensued thereafter in J&K, I conclude saying that the situation was regained by the Indian army and the invaders were pushed back with heavy losses.

US Aid to Pakistan

Pakistan forsaw a great period of difficulty ahead of the young nation and asked the US for aid. In 1954 Pak and USA signed the mutual Defence Assistance Agreement while in the same period India chose to remain non-aligned.

In 1954, US gave out open support to Pakistan in terms of money, construction work, Patton tanks, F-86 fighter aircrafts, rader equipment, guns to upgrade the existing war machine of Pakistan which were of second world war vintage. Fully realizing India's policy of non-alignment and non-aggression, Pakistan devoted full time in training and reorganising its armed forces with the help of US and generally all its borders were manned by para military forces. The military balance of power had been altered to Pakistan's advantage. Pakistan was given sufficient military hardware by US to raise, train and equip a strike force.

Role of Islam

The faith of Islam was brought to India in the 8th century AD by the Arab traders and principally by Turkish invaders knifing through the vulnerable North West. For one thousand years the Hindus lived under despotic and often cruel muslim rule. However muslim community sank to secondary position under the British rule. Muslim of the sub-continent in large measure are the descendants of converted Hindus and are therefore have similar looks, except in beliefs and some externals. The Turkish conquerers converted the Hindus partly by sword and mainly by persuation. They preached quality and thereby led an early revolution against caste system upon which Hinduism is based. The outcasts who had no standing in traditional society, turned for relief to the new religion of Islam.

But after partition, Pak descent into radicalism began on 12 March 1949 when constituent Assembly passed its objectives Resolutions declaring Pak as Islamic State. This surprised its Hindu members (Bengalis from East Pak) who had been assured publically by Mr. Jinnah that the new nation would be indifferent to religion. But Islam, since partition has influenced the entire population and government in Pak; Islam was of course the main bases of partition of British India.

3

Pak Becomes an Independent Sovereign State

Pak was carved out in a desperate urgency. It came into existance with horrible loss of lives and property and the migration of millions of dazed and destitute men, women and children. The cost was heavy in terms of human sufferings. But what the muslims wanted and what they achieved was a homeland of their own. They now had the freedom to worship, practice their religious faith and develop their culture. Moreover independence had opened up a bright future for the muslims who looked for a better standard of living, economic development, prosperity and a free life. But it seemed in those early years (1947-58) that the immense sacrifices might have been in vain for the Pak had been struggling from one crises to another, fighting to ward off the multiple problems that threatened the nation. The main problems were refugees, Indus water and Accession of the princely states.

The commission set up soon after partition, defined boundaries which resulted in many tragic events. Thousands of families were caught unaware. This resulted in hastened move across the border leaving the homes, property to seek refuge. This was followed by panic, fear and reprisals. Both the countries were soaked in blood. It left millions of refugees on either side of the border who had to be rehabilitated. It was generally felt in Pak that the commission was biased against Pak.

The waters of river Jhelum, Chenab and Indus were given to Pak under the Indus Basin Treaty. The treaty allowed for a transitional period for 10-13 years, after which the three Eastern rivers would fall exclusively to India's share and three Western rivers to Pak. During that period Pak would construct a system of replacement works consisting of dams, barrages and link canals financed by the Indus Development Fund.

Prior to partition there existed in British India many semi autonomous states whose future had to be settled before the Britishers left the country finally. There were some 560 such states all over the sub continent. On 25 July 1947, Lord Mountbatten (the last Viceroy of India) advised accession should be based on communal composition and geographical location. Nearly all the states accepted this and opted either for India or Pak accordingly. There were four states, Junagarh, Hyderabad, Jodhpur and Kashmir which did not agree to this arrengement.

The muslims of sub continent had finally achieved their goal to have an independent State for themselves. The muslims faced a lot of problems immediately after independence. However they managed to overcome most of those. Thus Pak came into existance as a dominion within the Commonwealth in Aug 1947, with Mr. Jinnah as Governor General and Mr. Liaquat Ali Khan as the Prime Minister, with West and East Pak separated by more than 1000 miles. Of all the well organised provinces of British India only the areas of Sindh, Baluchistan and North West Frontier Province (NWFP) were merged with Pak. The Punjab and Bengal were divided and Kashmir became a disputed territory.

However the separation in 1947 of British India into muslim State of Pak (with East and West wings) and Hindu India was never satisfactorily resolved; even till date.

Mohammad Ali Jinnah

Mr. Jinnah was over six feet tall, weighing less than 140 pounds. The sharp bones of determined face struck over hellow cheeks, he suffered from chronic bronchitis and died of lung cancer. He was strong, aristocratic and icy even in the worst heat, always wearing carefully tailored savile row suits and frequently sponting a monocle. Arrogant, yet honest, insulting but sensitive to the slightest personal snub; a revolutionary who disdained the mob and its sweaty, violent protests. Mr. Jinnah still remains mysterious, for no one knows with certainty the source of drive which shattered a continent.

His father was a Hindu but he was born in Karachi as a muslim. Mr. Jinnah himself revealed no particular religious devotion. In 1892, at the age of 18, he began law studies in England. After finishing his law, he returned to Bombay for practice. Ten years later he joined Congress party and later Muslim League.

He was basically a secular liberal who had studied and practised law. For such a man the muslim cause which inescapably bound up with Islam, embraced nationalism and patriotism as well as the strict meaning of religion. He wanted to see Pak as an embodiment of dynamic and forward looking Islam. According to Mr. Jinnah, the demands and struggle for Pak had been ensured mainly because there was danger of denial of basic rights to muslims in Hindu dominated India.

Soon after partition he said in March 1948 at Chittagong that the story of Pak, its struggle and achievements is the very story of great human ideals, struggling to survive in the face of odds and difficulties.

He was given the title of 'Quaid-i-Azam'.

Mr Jinnah, who worked very hard to see Pak as an independent and sovereign state, was ill for a long time even at the time of partition and died on 11 Sep 1948 due to his illness. Mr. Nizamudin who was then the Chief Minister of province of East Bengal since independence, was appointed governor general in place of Mr. Jinnah.

Liaquat Ali Khan

He was the first Prime Minister of independent Pak from 1947 to 1951. His contribution to the struggle were immense. Being the first PM of the country, he had to face number of serious problems to get the country in proper shape. His contribution in setting up administration and outlining foreign policies alongwith Mr. Jinnah was remarkable. He prepared a objective resolution, a prelude to future constitution for Pak.

During his tenure, India and Pak agreed to resolve the dispute of Kashmir in a peaceful manner through the efforts of UN. According to the agreement a ceasefire was affected in Kashmir in 1948. It was decided that a free and impartial plebicite would be held under the supervision of UN. After the death of Mr. Jinnah, he tried to fill the vaccume created. The problem of religious minorities again surfaced which was sorted out by him in consultation with Mr. Jawahar Lal Nehru, the PM of India.

He also established a National Bank of Pak in November 1949 and a paper mill in Karachi.

Mr. Liaquat Ali was assassinated in 16 October 1951. He was given the title of Shaheed-i-Millat.

Period upto Oct 1958

Under the newly framed constitution of Pak, the executive powers lay with the prime minister (PM). When Mr. Liaquat Ali Khan was assassinated on 16 Oct 1951, Khawaza Nizamudin who was the governor general at that time, was appointed as the second PM of Pak. He remained in power till he was removed in April 1953 by Mr. Ghulam Muhammad. Ghulam Muhammad was the governor general at that time. He wanted to change the status quo of executive powers. He then appointed Mohd. Ali Bogra an unknown person from East Pak as PM and dissolved the constituent assembly.

After coming to power as PM, Mr. Bogra set a new precedence of making C-in-C, Pak army as the Defence Minister of the country. This was the beginning of affording taste of power to the military leaders in Pak.

Mr. Mohd Ali Bogra, as the PM of Pak, worked very hard to settle the Kashmir problem in consultation with Mr. Nehru, the PM of India. It was during Mr. Bogra's tenure that Pak became the member of SEATO.

However before the Constitution of Pak could be finalized, Mr. Ghulam Mohd, the governor general of Pak dissolved the assembly, however Mr. Bogra was allowed to continue as the PM till next elections. This was done to counter the bill curtailing the powers of governor general.

In 1955, Mr. Ghulam Mohd., the governor general was forced to resign and Major General Iskander Mirza was made the acting governor general of Pak. The acting governor general Mr. Iskander Mirza dissmissed Mr. Bogra on 08 Aug 1955 from the post of PM. Mr. Iskander Mirza was confirmed as the fourth governor general of Pak on 04 October 1955. In place of Mr. Bogra, Mr. Chaudhary Mohd Ali was appointed as the new PM on 11 Aug 1955.

Mr. Chaudhary Mohd Ali worked on framing the Constitution and it was finally enforced in Pak on 23 March 1956. The country was declared as Islamic republic of Pak and governor general, Mr. Mirza was sworn in as the first President of Pak. Soon after the adoption of the constitution, Mr. Huseyn Shaheed Shurawrdy became the PM on 12 September 1956. Thereafter Mr. Chundrigai was appointed acting PM as Mr. Suhrawrdy resigned. Mr. Chundrigai was also replaced by Mr. Malik Feroz Khan as the PM of Pak on 16 December 1957. It was rediculous to note that the appointment of PM of a country was made a joke in Pak.

The Constitution vested the executive powers in the President. The Constitution provided for a federal form of government in the country, the Constitution, however was flexible and the President had the powers to suspend the fundamental rights of the people in case of an emergency. The Constitution of 1956 short lived and on 07 october 1958, Martial Law was promulgated and the Constitution was abrogated.

As President Mr. Iskandar Mirza abrogated the constitution and declared Martial Law, the C-in-C, General Mohd. Ayub Khan became the Chief Martial Law Administrator (CMLA) on 07 October 1958. Under General Ayub Khan the new Constitution was brought into force in 1962, which advocated Presential form of government with absolute powers vested in the President. The President had the power to dissolve the national assembly. Federal form of government was introduced and most of the powers were reserved with the central government. When General Ayub Khan handed over to General Yahya Khan, Martial Law was again inforced and Constitution was terminated on 25 March 1969.

Mr. Iskandar Mirza who himself was an army officer, was of the firm view that democratic institutions could not flourish in Pak due to lack of training in democracy and low literacy rate of masses. He wanted a controlled democracy for Pak with more powers with civil bureaucracy. He thought that politicians should be given powers to make policies but not to be allowed to interfere in the country administration.

4

FIELD MARTIAL MOHD. AYUB KHAN (1958-1969)

General Ayub Khan was the first Martial Law Administrator of Pak from 1958 to 1962 and thereafter he remained President of Pak from 1962 to 1969.

He was born on 14 May 1907 in an army family and his father was a Risaldar Major in Hodson's Horse. He was from a ruler background and had to walk upto four miles to his school from his village Rehana in Hazara district. After passing his matriculation in 1922, he was sent to Aligarh University. However before he could finish graduation, he was selected for Royal Military College at Sandhurt (England) in 1926. He was commissioned in the army in 1928. He fought in Second World War. During the Partition of India he was a Brigadier and opted to join the Pak army. Being the senior most army officer in Pak army, his status was raised to four Star General and was appointed as Commander-in-Chief (C-in-C) of the Pak army.

In 1954, when he was C-in-C, he was inducted into Mohd. Ali Bogra Federal Cabinet as Defence Minister. This marked the beginning of military involvement into the politics of Pak. General Ayub Khan played a key role in getting entry of Pak in UN sponsered alliance CENTO and SEATO.

On 07 October 1958, Mr. Iskander Mirza enforced the first Martial Law administration, with the help of General Ayub Khan and General Ayub Khan became the CMLA. In due course he assumed the charge of President of Pak in addition to his role as Chief Martial Law Administrator. Later he upgraded himself as Field Martial. Since the people of Pak were fed up with instability of the government since 1947, were happy with the change.

His Contribution

Foreign Minister Ayub Khan realized that he could not rule the country under army authority for an indefinite period and had to get to civil rule under a proper constitution. He lifted martial law on 08 July 1962 and a new costitution was introduced. The Constitution had the presidential type of government and principles of basic democracy were introduced. Field Martial Ayub Khan continued as President of Pak till proper elections were held in 1965. He defeated his rival Fatima Jinnah and was elected as the President of Pak; Though people attribute his success to many reasons legal and illegal.

Ayub Khan showed stern and determined commitment to reforms of political institutions. He was committed to the concept of 'Guided Democracy' as he termed it. He committed himself to sweeping reforms and laid emphasis on improving the lot of rural population. He pledged himself to sweeping economic changes as a major step in national reconstruction. He achieved much better results during his period than could have been expected from a civilian leadership. He accepted western political traditions and needs.

From 1947 to 1958, Pak experienced numerous changes and uncertainties in running the country's administration. The political leadership of the infant nation suffered an early casulty with the death of Mr. Jinnah, the founding father of Pak, in 1948 and the assassination of Mr. Liaquat Ali Khan, the PM of Pak in 1951. Until 1958 political parties waxed, waned and occassionally disappeared. Political leaders argued, intrigued and reduced each other to minimal importance. The country was essentially run by the civil servants with the backing of the army. The search for the national identity was complicated by the fact that inherent in the faith of Islam, to which majority of people adhere is the belief that 'Religion prevades' all aspects of life, private or public. The secular State was unacceptable to many orthodox muslims. Other problems facing the nation during the first decade of its existance were disparities between East and West Wings of Pak in population, natural resources and the living standards. The nation was at the verge of disintegration.

The military coup on 07 October 1958 was hailed by public. Foreign Minister Ayub Khan brought an end to Parliamentary government, dismissed the Cabinet, abrogated 1956 constitution, abolished the political parties and closed the office of the PM. He became Chief Martial Law Administrator (CMLA) and after 20 days became the President and appointed a Presidential Cabinet. He proclaimed that his aim was to clear up the mess and to attack the problems of smuggling, black marketing and corruption. He also promissed to give the country a workable new constitution for effective democrary as suited to internal conditions of Pak.

He retained the national integration formula as envisioned by the 1956 constitution. He laid emphasis on moderanisation. He was concerned with creating confidence among the people in the destiny of Pak and with maximising the rate of economic growth. He ignored at first the need for a political party to carryout the long term task of nation building and instead chose civil servants to execute his plans for the economic growth.

Field Martial Ayub Khan recognised that the fate of the nation depended on solutions to many problems concerning national integration and unity. Under him land reforms were successfully accomplished. The rural reconstruction program was able to attract massive popular participation. The stagnent economy of the previous decade gave way to notable success. Ayub Khan also made it possible for per capita gross income to raise faster in East Pak then in the West Wing, thus reversing comparative growth rates. The same high rate of annual income was registered for East Pak in agriculture and manufacturing. Large number of industrial units were set up in East Pak. That record economic growth could only be achieved with dogmatic approach and political stability and preservation of Law and order in the country.

He laid lot of emphasis on industralization and encouragement to private sectors to establish industries. This opened lot of job opportunities. He introduced educational reforms to raise the education standard. In addition to land reforms he brought in administrative reforms and labour laws. It was during his regime that country's capital was moved from Karachi to Islamabad in 1962.

Field Martial Ayub Khan ruled Pak almost for ten years and his regime made some notable achievements but could not remove to basic problems of Pak society. His efforts to erase fuedal relationship by carrying out land reforms, did not fully succeed. He was a military ruler, but tried hard to bring in basic democracy by appointing democrats and union councilors who were the leaders of rural and urban areas around the country. He constituted the electoral college for presidential elections and for the elections to provincial and legislatures, created under the constitution promulgated by Ayub Khan in 1962. Ayub also promulgated an Islamic marriage and family law ordanance in 1961, imposing restrictions on polygamy and divorce and reinforced the inheritance rights of women and minors.

Field Martial Ayub Khan's philosophy was indebited to the Mughals traditions, his rule was similarly personalized. Ayub justified his assumption of military rule by citing the nation's need for stability and necessity for the army to play a crucial role in sorting out inefficient politicians. He used two methods of governing in the initial stages to establish himself, one to intimidate the politicians and use of constitutional institution for stability. Stern measures were used against the politicians. He involved special provisions the 'PRODA' under which anyone found guilty of corruption was disqualified for 15 years from the public office. The press and publications ordanance was ameded to specify broad conditions under which newspapers and other publications could be controlled or closed down. Trade organisations and students groups were closely monitored and cautioned to avoid political activitics. The religious leaders (IMAMS) were warned against using political matters in religious gatherings. He was generally fair to the East wing of Pak. He only posted civil servants who were from the East as against earlier policy where civil servants from west were dominating in both the wings. He also introduced tax concessions to investments in less developed areas. The measure had important consequences in bringing industry to Punjab and gave incentive to small scale industries.

The 1962 constitution retained some aspects of Islamic nature of republic but omitted the word 'Islamic' in its original version; under protest Ayub added this word later. This meant that the President of Pak would be muslim and the advisory Council of Islamic ideology and Islamic Research Institute were established to assist the government in reconciling all legislations of the Quran and Sunna. Their function was advisory and their appointments were cleared by the President, so that the Ulemas had no influence in the order of the country.

In his foreign policy, he sought to improve and normalize relations with the neighbours, ie. India, China and Soviet Union. While retaining and renewing the alliance with US, he emphasized the preference for friendship and not subordination and bargained hard for higher returns to Pak. On the water dispute with India, he reached a compromise in 1960 which satisfied both the countries. This was approved and accepted by the world bank also. This enunciated that Indus, Jhelum and Chenab rivers be allocated to Pak and Ravi, Beas and Sutlez rivers be given to India.

As far as China was concerned, Ayub Khan got close to them particularly after Indo-Sino war of 1962.

He had a border agreement in March 1963 which included construction of highway connecting the two countries at Karakoram pass and also economic assistance and military equipment to Pak including nuclear technology. Soviet Union however did not approve of such a Sino-Pak diplomatic ties and moves.

Pak-Afgan Border Clash - 1961

Armed Tribal incursions from Afganistan in Pak border area began with the transfer of power in 1947 and it became a continued irritant for the Pak regime. Many Afgans had rendered the 19th century Anglo-Afgan border treaties as void and were trying to redraw the borders with Pak and were trying to create an independent nation Pakhtunistan. Pak was continuously involved in securing its borders. The relations between Pak and Afganistan touched very low when Pak embassy in Kabul was closed. Pak used US arms to deal with Afgan's intrusion which were primarily given for the purpose of fighting communism, which was not liked by US, since Afgans tilted towards Soviet Camp.

Indo-Pak War 1965

After J&K operations in 1947-48 the forces on both sides remained deployed along the ceasefire line, though actual hostilities between the two countries had come to halt. But cattle lifting, raids and regular ceasefire violations by Pak kept the area surcharged with tension. The US aid to Pak under the 1954 agreement, gave new boost to Pak war machinary and it raised confidence of their armed forces. As per the agreement US was to train and equip Pak new raisings army units so to prepare them against the Communist expansion. Since the threat from the Communist countries was nowhere to be seen and such a massive aid to Pak gave them the idea of new venture against India. This began in early 1965 when Field Martial Ayub Khan, the President of Pak visited China and he was presumably assured by the Chinese to support them in the event of war against India.

At the beginning of 1965, Pak faced certain formidable problems in nation building. They had received lot of aid from US, but the immediate challenge were immense. The future of Pak under army rule was precarious. India on the other hand was doing well all around. After the death of the Nehru, who was considered indispensable as PM of India by the whole nation, the transfer of authority was accomplished without dislocation or upheaval, by nominating Mr. Lal Bahadur Shastri as the PM of India.

The Shastri government attempted in general to prepetuate Nehru's policies on major foreign and domestic affairs. The economy was expanding, Mr. Shastri had not established his position as the new PM nor had he attempted to do so. He was well known in India, but the world did not know him much. He was known for his simplicity of living, yet he was firm and decisive.

Domestically Pak was restless, uneasy and divided beneath its economic pressure and progress. Ayub revived anti-India propaganda in an attempt to create cohesiveness. Pak press launched anti India campaign which was pursued relentlessly and vehemently before the war. Pak leaders themselves matched the velemence of the strongly controlled press. By contrast Indian officials were remarkably restrained and the Indian Press was moderate.

The military conflict actually began in the spring of 1965, with a test of strength in the improbable area of Rann of Kutch. Pak laid claims on certain areas in Rann of Kutch. Tension built up but it did not escalate into war, but troops stayed put in the battle location. However probing actions between lightly manned rival police forces opened in January 1965, which continued till April 1965. This campaign on part of Pak was intended to test its weapons and political climate in the country. Pak used US supplied patton tanks and other US arms for the first time and apparently escaped reprisals from US for employing weapons those had been supplied to them primarily to be used against communist expansion force. Pak also drew Indians into a unfavourable battle positions in that area where rainy season had set in and Pak had distinct logistical advantage and made some local gains. Pak evidently concluded from all these that it was politically and militarily capable of attacking a strong rival and improve his security concerns. Pak was not even deterred by brief

Indian action in Kargil in May 1965, where indians occupied offensive positions by securing dominating heights. These positions were tectically very important for Indian forces in Kargil.

In Pak, Field Martial Ayub, a military ruler evidently assumed a dominant role in military strategy. He did not need Parliamentary sanction for his actions. Infact he was fully supported by the people of West Pak. Pak thus shifted its emphasis and interest to North and J&K. Pak infiltrated large number of well trained and well armed personnel into J&K under operation code name as 'Zibalter'. The main infiltration force was organised at Murree (West Pak) in 26 May 1965. It was composed of 30,000 man, fully equiped and armed to infiltrate into J&K. Maj. General A.H. Malik, Goc 12 Infantry Division (Pak) was made the commander of this operation. The troops mainly were from Azad Kashmir with a mix of Mujahideen and Razakars. These people were infiltrated into entire J&K through the infrequented routs. Their main aim was to advance to State of J&K, Srinagar. These infiltrators were first noticed in area of Mandi near Poonch on 05 August 1965. OP Zibralter was planned to carryout sabotage in support of main Pak operation which were to be launched after its success. However this operation failed miserably and these infiltrators were caught mostly with the help of locals on who Pak was heavily depending. Though Pak vehemently denied that there was no infiltration from their side and that these were the local Kashmiries themselves who revolted against the Indian rule. But there was enough evidence for the world to believe that Pak did initiate hostilities by way of infiltration in J&K.

Indian army quickly responded by crossing the ceasefire line to the North and NE and capturing Strategic positions, a short distance inside Azad Kashmir, the Pak held portion of the State. These moves were necessary in part as Indian contended to close off main infiltration or invasion routes into Indian Kashmir. This also gave Indian forces an offensive position to threaten Azad Kashmir and impose caution on Pak ill designs. The operation to clear. Haji-Pir Pass (opposite Uri Sector) which Pak had occupied was also carried out. Some other posts along the ceasefire line were also cleared. The Kashmiris did not support the Pak as was expected by them.

Since 'Op Zibralter' failed, Pak opened a new front on 01 September 1965 against Chhamb sector. With application of large size force, their aim was to capture Akhnoor in a Swift and surprise move and cut off road Jammu-Akhnoor-Rajauri-Poonch. They nearly succeeded and captured Chhamb and Jaurian by 05 September 1965, which are very close to strategic Akhnoor bridge over river Chenab. After initial reverses, the situation was stablized by Indian forces. India then opened a new front in Punjab by 11 corps and then in Sialkot-Chawinda by 1 Corps. This move by

Indian troops paid handsome dividents and Pak suffered heavily on these fronts. However India lost Chhamb to Pak.

US had imposed arms embargo on both India and Pak during the War, but it hurt Pak more since they did not have spares for their aircrafts and tanks. Pak's ill designs were forestalled by the Indian forces and ceasefire was declared. Pak defence journal remarked that the war was a failure for Pak since its strategic objective of liberation of Kashmir was not achieved, resulting in psychological gain for India.

The Indian military circle strongly opposed acceptance of a premature ceasefire, particularly in view of Pak's gain in Chhamb and Jaurian Sectors. They wanted to cripple Pak's armour in Punjab sector sufficiently to reduce the possibility of another major attack by Pak in near future. As reported by Mr Selig S. Harrison in Washington Post of 14-15 Sep 1965 that Indian Cabinet was divided over the timings of a truce during 'U Thant' visit in this connection. General Chaudhary, the Chief of Army Staff reportedly urged the Cabinet on 13 September 1965 to avoide cessation of hostilities at that point. The army at that point was at the verge of a decisive victory in Punjab and should be allowed to inflict the maximum damage on the Pak war machinery. During the debate in Indian Parliament, the arguement was advanced that Pak would probably reject a ceasefire at that time and India by accepting one, whould have to chance to stigmatise her adversary in the world opinion for continuing the war. On this basis the Indian army accepted the ceasefire.

The invasion by Pak in 1965, was partly an aggressive design to solve the Kashmir problem by force, partly it appeared a preventive war against India's perspective strength. In attacking India, much bigger than its own size, Pak demonstrated that the whole nation can be driven to Jehad or holy war under Islam to fight when necessary even if the cause is hopeless.

Tashkent Conference

The conference began on 04 February 1966 among growing doubts that peaceful Indo-Pak solution was possible. The battle areas were still unspecified, economic relations were suspended and diplomatic contacts were negligible. For several weeks beforhand, Field Martial Ayub Khan and Mr. Shastri the PM of India had maintained public attitude of regidity with no signs of compromise. Mr. Shastri initially insisted that Kashmir could not be discussed at all and then modified to say that the question could be talked about, but not negotiated. Ayub insisted that a political settlement of Kashmir was the fundamental necessity and made this a pre requisite to a no-war agreement. India infact wanted to resolve such issue as withdrawal of forces without talking about Kashmir whereas Pak purpose was the unchanged desire to keep the Kashmir question alive.

The Tashkent declaration had the following clauses:-

(a) The two governments will make an effort to establish good relations between India and Pak in accordance with UN Charter.

(b) The PM of India and President of Pak agree to withdraw forces no later than 25 February 1966, to position held before 05 August 1964.

(c) Both India and Pak agree to follow the principles of non-interference in their affairs and will interference discourage the use of any propaganda against each other.

(d) Both countries also agree to open diplomatic functioning and return of High Commission to both the countries to their posts.

(e) Measures towards restoration of economic and trade relations, communication as well as cultural exchange between the two countries were to be taken.

(f) Pow, would be repatriated.

(g) Discussions would continue relating to problems of refugees, and eviction of illigal immigrants. Both sides will create conditions that will prevent mass exodus of people.

End of Field Martial Ayub Khan's Regime

The Indo-Pak war of 1965 cast some negative shadows on the performance of Mr. Ayub. People of Pak blamed him for his actions in Tashkent declaration. His close man Mr. Z.A. Bhutto also turned against him and launched own political party (PPP) with a aim to remove Ayub Khan from the power. Awamy League under Sheikh Mujibur Rehman was also raising its voice blaming him for his policies being against the Bengalis of East Wing. His policies to concentrate powers in his own hands, control over Press and Media and imposing emergency in the country attributed to end of his era. There were anti-Ayub movements by the people of Pak including students. Law and Order broke down and he had to step down on 25 March 1969. He handed over the powers to another militaryman, General Mohd Yahya Khan who was the c-in-c of Pak army at that time.

During the Tashkent conference Mr. Lal Bahadur Shastri, the PM of India died, which was a big loss to India once again, after Mr. Nehru's death.

5

GENERAL MOHD. YAHYA KHAN (1969-1971)

General Yahya Khan was born at Chakwal in February 1917. His father Saadat Ali Khan belonged to Peshawar, a family of Pashtun. After finishing his education in Punjab University, General Yahya Khan joined Indian Military Academy. He was commissioned in the Indian army on 15 July 1938 and joined 4/10 Baluch Regiment. His early postings were in NWFP. During World War II, he was in North Africa, Italy and Iraq. After partition of Pak, he played an important role in establishing Pak Staff College at Quetta.

During 1965, he commanded 7 Infantry Division (Pak). He became C-in-C of Pak army in 1966 with the rank of general.

In 1969 when there was agitations against Field Martial Ayub Khan, he decided to handover the reign of the country to another military man, General Yahya

Khan, the Pak army Chief. Immediately after coming to power, he declared martial law in the country on 25 March 1969 and assumed the title of Chief Martial Law Administrator (CMLA). He terminated the Constitution and dissolved the national and provincial assemblies on 31 March 1969 and then he became President of Pak.

Unlike others, he was not keen in prolonging his rule. He immediately started looking for options to restore the powers to the elected representatives of the country. On 29 March 1970, he through an ordanance presented an interim Constitution. It was a way out according to which the forthcoming elections were to be organised. It was during his tenure that general elections were held in December 1970.

The trouble started when the results of the elections were announced. The Awamy League under Sheikh Mujib Ur-Rehman, Swept 160, out of 162 seats allocated to East Pak. However this party failed to get even one seat from any province in West Pak. On the other hand Mr. Z A Bhutto's PPP emerged the single largest party from Punjab and Sindh and managed to win 81 national assembly seats, all from the West Pak. The split mandate resulted in a political chaos where neither Bhutto nor Rehman was prepared to accept his opponent as PM of the new elected assembly. As such the ball fell in General Yahya's court. He unfortunately handled the situation very badly. He used the armed forces to crush the elections related agitation in East

Pak. This was the beginning of bigger trouble to come, i.e. war of 1971.

Situation in East Pak

The Bengalis simmered over a number of accumulated grievances. They contended that East Pak despite its size was dominated by the West and treated as an economic step child. Many insisted that military revolution that changed Pak history, was actually launched because military rulers feared that they would come under Bengali rule, if the elections were held. The revolt forestalled the first scheduled general elections which the Bengalis contented would have swept the elections and Pak Parliament would have been dominated by the Bengalis. Throughout the government in Pak had been drawn from the West Pak. The East Pak further complained that while their jute produced most of Pak's foreign exchange, but the government spent dispropotionate share of the proceed in the west. Two third of the country's foreign exchange was earned by East Pak.

For the purpose of keeping tight control on the East wing, there was one officer from the West in each big village of the East Pak. There were disparities not only in economic spheres but also in appointment of administrative services and executive powers. These emotions kept Pak in the condition of semi devided uncertainty. The feeling was so pronounced that during

1965 operations Indian made no plans to attack the East Wing, because they knew that Bengalis hate the West Pak.

Since the results of the 1970 general elections did not allow West Pak to go ahead in formation of the central government, and East Pak was denied its right to do so, there were agitations to the effect. On 07 March 1971, Mr. Mujib Ur Rahman suggested following action on part of Chief Martial Administrator.

(a) Immediate Withdrawl of martial law

(b) Immediate withdrawl of all army personnel to barracks.

(c) Transfer of power to elected representation of the people.

(d) Immediate cessation of military build up and heavy inflow of military men to East Pak from the West wing.

(e) Immediate and total cessation of firing on the civilians.

(f) Non-interference by military personnel in functioning of government in East Pak and stop victimisation of employees.

(g) Maintenance of Law and order to be left to Police and Bengali EPR assited by, whereever necessary by Awamy League volunteers.

Lt. General Tikka Khan who was the governor of East Pak ordered on 10 April 1971 (Later changed) to disarm all East Bengal Regiment Battalions, the East

Pak rifles and the police. The security of naval bases and major cities was taken over. However Lt. General A.A. Niazi took over as the CMLA of East Pak soon thereafter.

Genocide in East Pak

General Yahya - Mujib constitution talks failed on 25 March 1971 and action against unarmed East Pak commenced the same night. Additional army troops were rushed to East Pak from the West Wing by ships and landed at Chittagong and Chalana and later dispersed in the areas of Dacca, Comilla and Jessore. General Yahya Khan called upon the armed forces to crush the freedom movement in East Pak. The police of East Pak were disarmed and the officers of East Bengal Regiment and rifles were taken prisoners.

The Pak army killed innocent men, women and children. Navy also took part in the fighting. Chittagong was shelled. Even Pak Airforce helicopters shelled populated areas of East Pak. It was also reported by one of the UNI correspondents, who toured the area that "Pak army is believed to have used" Napalm bombs in operation to crush people of East Pak. The orgy of mass murder, destruction, rape and looting indulged in by the Pak in Dacca alone put to shame the Nazi doings in Europe words are inadequate to express what Dacca experienced in these days, during the Pak troops acted as though in mad desperation".

As narrated by Vice Chancellor (VC) of Dacca University, Justice Abu Sayeed Chowdhary, "The women hostel in Dacca University was the vanue of the most blood curdling heineous crimes in recent times; The Pak troops entered the hostel and dragged the girls out of their rooms. There was panic and shrieks could be heard. Saris, Skirts, Salwars were ripped open and flung aside, next blouses, khameezs and brassiers were torn off and girls were physically lifted off by their breasts or hair — some held upside down. As they tried to cover their shame with their hands, the troops kicked them on their private parts with their heavy boots, punched them with their fists, some even bayoneted the delicate pubic portion, blood trickling therefrom. Next came raping. The girls cried, Shrieked and struggled but the beastly soldiers went on raping. Blood ran, as one after another girl was raped successively 10-12 times. Most of them fell unconscious as the troops departed after satisfying their devilish lust. The girls were in such a condition that they could not even cover up their bodies. It was at this juncture that 50 girls jumped to their death from the roof top.

There was another report by a correspondence of 'National Herald' on 18 April 1971 about massacre in Rajshahi, astride river Padma, "Padma looks like a river of sorrow, moaning and groaning with thousands of bodies on her breast. The deads were her kins, born and brought up on her banks. The dried up bed is also strewn with bodies. The dead has seen the Sun rise on Padma and now it is the Sun set to them. It is the tale of town crying in anguish on the bank of Padma. Rajshahi has fallen to Pak Marauders".

Mohd. Ali Jinnah and his friends in the Muslim League treated the people of East Pak like a child. They fed them with the ideas of the two nations theory, of the country with two wings. Then Field Martial Ayub Khan and General Yahya Khan tried to be tough with these people of East Pak. The people of the East Pak having been exploited for two decades or more at last woke up to the realities of the day and sought for certain freedom. General Yahya's genocide is thus without political purpose. It serves only as the last act in tragic history of Pak, which General Yahya Khan chose to write with the blood of people of East Pak.

Mr. Mujib-ur-Rehman was arrested on 25/26 March 1971 and open civil war broke out. PM of India had assured full support to Mujib for his struggle. As the rate of killings of civilians in East Pak by the Pak army increased, approximately ten million rufugees fled to India. Operations of Mukti Bahani caused severe casualities to Pak army. President, General Yahya Khan blamed India for the situation in East Pak and declared state of emergency in Pak on 23 November 1971. Bangladesh was finally liberated with over 90,000 Pak army personnel including General Niazi taken as POW by the Indian army.

Indo-Pak War 1971

On 03 December 1971, Pak aircrafts launched pre-emptive strikes on forward airfields of India in Punjab and J&K; thus declaring war on India. Indians were well prepared with superiority in every field. Bangladesh was liberated and adequate preparations had been made to meet such eventuality of Pak invading India. Some of the fierest battles were fought in J&K, Punjab of which important one were, battles of Basanter, Longewala and Chhamb. There were certain sectors where Indians did not expect Pak to repeat 1965 and Indian intelligence failed them about the impending Pak attack in Chhamb Sector; where India lost a little.

In the overall analysis Indian army performed extremely well and the result of the war was a clear cut victory for India. Indian army had captured approximately 5,500 Sq miles of area of Pak territory, which was later returned to them as per Shimla agreement signed in 1972, between the two governments ie India and Pak.

On sea, Indian Navy carried out attacks on Karachi port and destroyed one mine sweeper and two destroyers of Pak navy. The Indian navy also ensured security of Eastern Coast. These operations were carried out under 'OP Trident' and 'OP PYTHON' respectively. The Indian Airforce also did a commendable job by destroying Pak aircrafts at Dacca airfield itself in the Eastern Wing thereby rendering Pak airforce totally incapable of any operations in East Pak. Indian Airforce maintained total air superiority in the Western theatre throughout the war.

The venture by Pak in December 1971 proved disasterous to them since it resulted in break up of Pak and emergence of independent State of Bangladesh. It was proved that religion alone can not become the basis of sustenance of a nation.

Mr. Z A Bhutto was still hopeful that Mr. Mujib ur Rehman who had been allowed to go in exile to England, would be willing to talk to political leaders of West Pak, on return and help resolve the future of East Pak. He also thought that Mujib would denounce Indian aggression and act in the best interest of Pak as a whole. But Mujib who was returning from England did not want to reach East Pak and enroute proclaimed 'Bangladesh' as a sovereign State. He denounced Pak, Quid-e-Azam, the people of Pak and their army. Before going anywhere he decided to go to Delhi where he met Mrs. Indira Gandhi, the PM of India.

This enormous folt was too much for the public of West Pak. The main blame was placed on the doors of the armed forces. The armed forces themselves were disillusioned and most bitter. The feeling of disgrace was rampant amongst them.

In the final analysis, it is abundantly clear that country (Pak) was forced into war without any national aim. It was fought without a purpose and with total lack of coordination between the civilian effort and the armed forces and amongst the three services. It was infact a classical demonstration as to how not to fight a war. The Indian victory was due to as much to their careful and patient planning as it was to the lack of all this in Pak. The Indian high command had assured victory by leaving enough margin for setbacks in the field; the Pak high command on the other hand had ensured own defeat even if its armed forces won all the tectical battles.

His Contributions (General Yahya Khan)

General Yahya Khan had inherited a country which was disunited. The popular, prolonged and widespread political agitation against President Ayub Khan and his government had devalued the administration and lowered its morale. The discipline of civil life had been eroded by prolonged political agitation. Regionalism and quasi nationalism raised hands. The polarisation particularly between East and West Pak which had been allowed to take root became pronounced. The gulf between the two wings threatened to grow wider and deeper.

The Chief Martial Law Administrator ruled the country and enjoyed the previlleges of Presidency of Pak. Field Martial Ayub Khan got generally cut off from the armed forces and ruled through bureaucracy. General Yahya Khan though had the Headquarters of CMLA, but he surrounded himself with a few senior army officers, who had no responsibilities in the governance, but they did influence his major decisions. They were being referred to as the Coterie'.

When General Yahya Khan came into power in March 1969, he involved army particularly officers more and more in civil administration and other duties of political nature. The armed forces, particularly army got spurt of promotions. The member of higher ranks were doubled overnight without proper boards or commission, this incapable lot occupied higher and responsible posts. When armed forces become supreme in the country, there could be no accountability for their actions, good or otherwise.

In an attempt to make his regime more acceptable, General Yahya, dismissed almost 300 senior civil servants and identified 30 families those were said to control about half of Pak GNP. To curb their power, Yahya issued an ordanance in 1970 against monopolies and restrictive trade practices. He also made committment to shift power to civil government but in the process of making this shift, his intended reforms broke down.

General Yahya Khan energetically started reorganising the Pak army soon he took over. He has been forgotton for his positive contributions towards national building and only being remembered and repeatedly being criticized for his negative qualities.

When Field Martial Ayub Khan handed over the reign of the country to him on 25 March 1969, he inherited lot of constitutional problems of inter provincial ethnic rivalry between Pathan - Punjabis - Mujahirs who dominated West Pak and ethnic muslims of East Pak. He was forced to perform multiple role of caretaker head of Pak, i.e. drafting a constitution and managing the Pak army as C-in-C. All these were complex problems since 1948. He sincerely attempted to solve Pak constitutional and inter provincial rivalries and other linked problems. Although correct in principles but was too late in timings and served only to further intensify the political polarisation between West and East Pak.

He was a very competent army officer, from a well to do family background. His shortcomings in functioning as the supreme commander that became evident in 1971 Indo-Pak war, could not have been known in 1966. It appears that Yahya's sect and ethnicity may have played a part in Ayub's decision to select him as the C-in-C of Pak army. General Musa writes in his memoirs that Yahya was not his first choice as army C-in-C but was selected by Ayub, overruling General Musa's reservations about Yahya's character and habits of over drinking and disliking the tea totallers. He liked courtesans, but his passion was listening to music and dance. This further shows that Ayub picked him as C-in-C on other considerations than merit. Altas Gauhar, Ayub's close confidant described 'Yahya as one selected in preference to other competent generals, because Yahya, who had come to hit the bottle head, had no time for politics and was considered as harmless and loyal person by Ayub.

Though as C-in-C under Field Martial Ayub Khan, General Yahya Khan was instrumental in getting arms aid from China since Ayub had no time for the defence or the army. Soon after the war had started in 1965, US had imposed embargo on both India and Pak. This adversely affected Pak army. Pak then turned towards China for military aid and the Chinese tank T-59 started replacing US, M-47/48 tanks. First batch of 80 X T-59 tanks arrived in Pak in 1965-66. Three more infantry divisions, largely equipped with Chinese equipment were raised by 1968. General Yahya also had two more corps Headquarters i.e. 2 corps and 4 corps raised during his tenure as the C-in-C Pak army.

Soon after partition, Mr. Jinnah adopted a policy to make army a national army and ordered immediate raisings of two battalions of Bengali muslims in 1948. This was reversed by Ayub Khan, who became the C-in-C in January 1951. Yahya paid for the sins of all those ruled Pak from 1951-69. The defeat of Pak army in 1971 was not an individual failure but failure of a system with flawed constitution, geography, philosophy, military and conceptual foundations.

The End of Era

General Yahya Khan, as the President as well the C-in-C of Pak army failed to plan the war of 1971. This ultimately resulted in defeat of Pak, dismemberment of the country and 90,000 personnel of West Pak were taken as POW in East Pak by the Indian army. Surrender of Pak forces without much resistance and fall of Dacca made Yahya Khan the greatest villain in Pak. Anger over this humilating defeat by India boiled into street demonstrations throughout Pak. Rumours of impending Coup d'etat by junior army officers against the government of Yahya Khan swept the country. People from all walks of life started criticising him and thus he was left with no other option than to handover powers to the leader of Pak Peoples Party (PPP).

Mr. Z A Bhutto bacame the President of Pak on 20 December and he placed General Yahya Khan under house arrest in 1972.

General Yahya Khan died on 10 August 1980 in Rawalpindi.

After liberation of Bangladesh Pak was left with only four provinces of West Pak; Sindh, Punjab, NWFP and Baluchistan. The defeat suffered by the armed forces of Pak was not a result of a military factors alone but had been brought about as the accumulative result of political, international, moral and military factors. The political development that took place between 1947-1971 included the effects of two martial law periods, hastened the process of political and emotional isolation of East Pak from the West which was all powerful.

The loss of East Pak had some positive effects on the progress of Pak. By shedding the poorest province with large number of dissidents, Pak was able to concentrate on the West Wing more effectively. The problem of maintenance and governing two separate wings also vanished and so was the role of Pak in South East Asia. The security situation had changed remarkably. Any illusion of parity vis-a-vis India were demolished. Although both China and US tilted towards Pak politically, but none of these could influence India's position since it had already signed a friendship treaty with the Soviet Union. The Shimla agreement in 1972 restored most of the Status quo ante the 1971 war.

6

Mr. Z.A. Bhutto

Pak People's Party (1971-1977)

He was born on 05 January 1928. He did his early education in Bombay. In 1947 he joined the University of California. In 1950, after finishing his degree with honours, he was admitted in Oxford. Returning to Pak with a law degree from Oxford he practised law and also was a lecturer on International law in Muslim Law College Sindh, his home town.

He married Nusrat Sphahani on 08 September 1951. Benazir was born on 21 January 1953 as his first child. A tall dashing and well dressed, he looked like a man of dedicated inflexibility. In 1958, he joined General Iskander Mirza's Cabinet as commerce minister, later Ayub's ministry in 1963 as foreign minister. He was instrumental in getting Ayub close to establishing closer economic and diplomatic ties with Turkey and Iran. Though he left Ayub in 1966 due to difference of opinion over Tashkent agreement after the Indo-Pak war 1965.

Bhutto launched his own political party 'Pak Peoples Party (PPP) soon after leaving Ayub. During 1970 general elections PPP won a large number of seats in West Pak, but Mr Sheikh Mujib ur Rehman of the East Wing who had larger majority of his seats than Mr Bhutto, did not let Bhutto alone enjoy the victory as was the practice earlier by West Pak. This led to difference of serious opinion and a political stalemate in the country. General Yahya Khan tried to control law and order in both the wings of his country, but failed since patience of people, particularly of the Bengalis who suffered at the hands of politicians from West Pak, had been exhausted. Military leadership had been discredited. People were no longer prepared to accept an inefficient government. The public severely criticized and accused General Yahya Khan for his government's ineptness and liability that culminated with 1971 national debacle.

General Yahya Khan sensing the turmoil in the country handed over the powers to the Z A Bhutto, the leader of the most popular party of West Pak at that time, on 20 December 1971. Mr. Bhutto became the President of Pak. He inherited a disturbed and disperate nation. In an address to the sick nation, he promised to build a new Pak.

Since Bangladesh became a separate independent State and it was recognised by large number of countries including Britain and other Western countries, Bhutto withdrew from Commonwealth Nations and SEATO, expressing his annoyance.

On 02 July 1972, he signed the Shimla agreement with India which resulted in repatriation of 90,000 Prisoners of War of Pak and return of occupied land by either side.

Due to his strong hand dealings, the public felt victimised by his rule and following political crisis, General Zia ul Haq, who was the C-in-C of Pak army, took over the reigns from him and imposed martial law on 05 July 1977.

After the promulgation of 1973 Constitution, Mr Bhutto became the Prime Minister of Pak. He advocated democracy and modified federal and Parliamentary system.

Mr. Bhutto carried out lot of land reforms, though his own holdings were affected and nationalized the industries. He also nationalized all the banks. He was an able politician and a good administrator. He got most of the Islamic countries to attend Islamic Summit in Lahore on 22 Feb 1974. Bhutto was a very popular leader in Pak. He came up through student power in the country. He mobalized the country's youth to overthrow President Ayub Khan and Steadily built up his mass appeal. In the elections of 1970 and 1977 he proved that noone in West Pak could come anywhere near him.

As foreign minister Bhutto inadvertantly became the principal spokeperson for a new attitude of defiance against the West which characterised the new Pak line. He carried this aspect of campaign to logical conclusion by threatening to withdraw from the UN unless it was supported on Kashmir. Bhutto also became the principal figure in widening efforts to win support from China. He was sharply attacked for his Pro-China policy even in Pro-Pak circles in Kashmir.

He was assisted by General Zia ul Haq after 1977 elections since there were bloody protest by the main opposition party, the Pak National Alliance (PNA), who alleged rigging in the elections and had lost badly to Bhutto's PPP. The rioting in April-May 1977 forced General Zia to take over the Country's governance. General Zia ul Haq was the Army Chief of Pak at that time. Despite proclaimed misrule during Bhutto's time, General Zia noticed with concern, Bhutto's mass appeal was still intact, hence he postponed the planned elections and put Mr Bhutto behind the bars.

During the last year of his rule, Bhutto had alienated the top elite in almost every sphere of life in the country, the army, judiciary, administration, the learned professionals and businessmen by his sheer arrogance. After he was overthrown and put in jail, he was charged for killing an opponent's father. He was sentenced to death and same was confirmed by the Supreme Court of Pak.

Number of countries urged General Zia not to carryout the sentence. Though India kept silent, but China, US, Soviet Union, Iran, Saudi Arabia, Egypt, Libya and number of other countries advised General Zia for mercy. But soon after the announcement of death penalty for Bhutto, the events in Iran, went against him. The Shah of Iran who had some say in the politics of Pak, was removed. With the development even Saudi Arabia felt insecured and did not openly go against a military ruler on the flank. Some of the other Islamic powers who were friendly to Pak and wanted stability and peace in that country also advised Zia not to execute Bhutto, who was a popular leader of international fame and had the mass following as such could set Pak ablaze and ruin his own future. They even reported to have offered to keep Bhutto for a life term in their country, so to ensure his inaccessibility to Pak's internal politics.

General Zia rejected these proposals because in the first place he did not trust the people of Pak who could betray Bhutto, could do so with him also and secondly, the countries who offered for the life long custody of Bhutto did not enjoy safety of their own thrones. Zia knew if Bhutto came back he would be ten times more potent against Zia and possibly be in power the next day. If Bhutto came to power, Zia knew, then either it would be his neck or Bhutto's since as per Bhutto, General Zia had already committed 'High Treason' punishable by death. Zia therefore tried to save his neck.

General Zia tried to play the propaganda in the public. As soon as Bhutto went to Supreme court for appeal against his death sentence, the Pak government published and widely circulated 'white paper' giving out that charges against Mr Bhutto were authentic. The aim was to prejudice the minds of the people of Pak against Bhutto, to seek to generate hatred and resentment against him, to demolish his image. This was part of assiduous endeavour which was started against Mr Bhutto covertly and overtly from 05 July 1977 onwards.

Bhutto's ambition to make Pak a nuclear weapon country is not open to doubts. After India exploded a nuclear device at Pokhran in May 1974, Bhutto said, "Eat grass to produce the bomb." He was able to negotiate an agreement with France which would have given Pak a nuclear reprocessing plant, which was capable of producing weapons grade plutonium. There was tremendous pressure from US on Pak and France not to go ahead with the agreement. Bhutto who was more adament, invited negative reaction from US, including being deprived of his throne. The irrationality of Bhutto's nuclear amibition was the biggest question mark which hung over his allegations that General Zia scuttled the procession plant in return for foreign backing for his coup.

But the historians are still surprised as to why did Mr Bhutto, a man who had power, popularity, a highly educated and an intellectual of high rating, liberal up bringing and highly capable of deciding what was good for him and went wrong in his dealings. If he had retained the loyalty of those who had served him well and not twisted every instrument of power that he could lay hand on, no ambitious general could have dared to throw him out of power since he was popular and had the mass following.

Bhutto to keep control over the army purged the military ranks of about 1400 officers soon on taking over the reigns of Pak. He also created a para military force called the 'Federal Security Force', which functioned as a personal security guard for him, a watchdog on the armed forces and as an internal security force. A white paper issued in 1976 on Defence, firmly suboardinated the armed forces to civilian control and gave Bhutto the decisive voice in all matters relating to National Security of Pak.

After 1971 Indo-Pak war, a diminshed Pak began to rearrange its national life under the leadership of Mr Bhutto. Bhutto moved decisively to restore national confidence and pursued an active foreign policy, taking a lead role in Islamic and third world forums. Although Pak did not join the non-aligned movement until 1979, the position of Bhutto's government coincided largely with that of non-aligned nations. Domestically, Bhutto pursued a populist agenda and nationalized major industries and banking system. In 1973, he promulgated a new Constitution accepted by the most political parties and he relinquished the presidency to become PM. Although Bhutto continued with his populist and socialist rhetoric, he increasingly relied on Pak urban industrialists and rural landlords. Over a period the economy stagnated largely as a result of the dislocation and uncertainty produced by Bhutto's frequently changing economic policies.

Though discontented, the army remained silent for some time. Bhutto's nationalization program and land reforms further earned him the enemity of the entrepreneurial and capitalist class, while religious leaders saw in his socialism an enemy of Islam. His decisive flaw, however was to deal constructively with the opposition. His rule grew heavy handed. In general elections in 1977, nine opposition parties united in the Pak National Alliance' (PNA) against his own party, PPP. They alleged rigging in elections and organised demonstrations throughout the country which led to his downfall and military take over.

After the rule of two military rulers ie. Ayub and Yahya Khan, Bhutto also proved a civilian dictator. A champion of poor and downtrodden, he had no patience for the dilatory dictates and democratic debate. He introduced his own constitution duly providing the democratic and Parliamentary type of government. In trying to sweep away all obstacles in his way, he assumed presidential powers and then came around to devise a constitution in which the PM became the Chief Executive and the President was assigned the ceremonial role. Bhutto also decided not to lift the emergency which had been imposed during the

Bangladesh war and infact suspended the fundamental rights, on the pretext of consideration of security. Bhutto himself did not live upto the standards of his own Constitution and allowed his feudal and autocratic nature to violate its spirits as and when he found it expedient to do so.

During Bhutto's rule a serious rebellion also took place in Afganistan and led to harsh suppression of Baloch rebels with purported assistance from the Shah of Iran. Subsequently, successionist uprisings in Balochistan were put down by the martial law administrator General Zia ul Haq.

Bhutto's move were laudable but fell short in performance. His near monopoly of decision making power prevented democratic institutions from taking roots.

His over reaching ambitions managed to antagonise all but his close allies and friends. Bhutto's power derived less from the 1973 Constitution then from his charismatic appeal to the people and from the vigour of the PPP. Its socialist program and Bhutto's oratory had done much to radicalize the urban sectors in the late 1960s and were responsible for the popular optimism accompanying the restoration of democracy.

Bhutto was also able to mobalize Support for a drive against Baloch. The main grievance of Baloch was setting of Punjabis in the rich resources land. The long dormant crisis erupted in 1973 into an insurgency that lasted four years. This was put down by Pak army using even brutal methods and equipment provided by Iran and helicopter gunships piloted by Iranians. Some of the insurgents had Communist leanings and some of the world countries were apprehensive that automonous and independent Balochistan might allow Soviet Union to develop and use port Gwadar, hence no one helped Baloch in their cause for independence. However General Zia took more moderate approach later relying more on economic development to placate the Baloch.

Mr Bhutto's contribution to nation building were tremendous. He bargained with India after 1971 Indo-Pak war and was party to Shimla agreement. He managed to get back 90,000 POW of Pak from India, who had surrendered during Bangladesh's war to Indian army in 1971. He also had US arms embargo lifted and got weapons from China. He invested over one and half billion dollars on armament and modernisation of defence forces. He established a separate Defence production and embarked upon defence collaboration with muslim States. This was Mr Bhutto who entered in establishment of Nuclear Reprocessing Plant agreement with France which though was shelved by General Zia ul Haq under pressure from US.

The warning that Mr Z A Bhutto gave to third world about the military rule was :-

> "Military Coup d'etats are the worst enemies of national unity. If it becomes permanent part of

> political infrastructure, it means the falling the last petal of the last withered rose, it means the end".

I also wish to give out the last feelings of late Mr Z A Bhutto, who was a great Stateman and a diplomat, contained in his book "If I am assassinated" just to highlight as to how a dictator (General Zia in this case) aims at eliminating the elite of the country for his own survival.

> "As I sit in the four walls of this tiny death cell, my mind reflects on the canvass of my life spent with dedication in the service of my people. My mind wonders over the rapidly changing contours of the magnificent political awakening. Man is moving towards revolution and reforms. He is determined to snatch his rights from the usurping order of exploitation. In my solitary confinement, I sometime think, I have lived the past twice over. The scenes that come on the screen of my memory are a veritable feast. I recall my momentous occasions: the partition, the rebellious mood of youth, the epic struggles, the Indo-Pak wars, the Security Council, the matching of wits with the giants. If out of the whole mosaic of the past, I have to select one piece from my most crucial and momentous achievements, I would not refer to the period when I picked up the broken pieces of an asundered land in 1971, nor the Shimla agreement. I would perhaps not refer to the blood, sweat and tears, I shed in seeking to create a society marked with equity and justice, my tireless efforts to bring a smile on the face and contentment in the

souls of people who had shed bitter tears since 'Moenjodaro' was built. In the light of recent developments which have taken place, my single most important achievement which I believe will dominate the potrait of my public life in an agreement which I arrived at after an assiduous and tenacious endeavour spanning over eleven years of negotiations. In the present context the agreement of mine, concluded in June 1976, will perhaps be my greatest achievement and contribution to the survival of one people and one nation."

He concluded with the quotation with which Jawahar Lal Nehru ended his book 'Discovery of India'. It is a quotation from Ostrovosky's 'How the Steel was Tempered" It says:

> "Man's dearest possession is his life and since it is given to him to live but once, he must so live as not to be scared with shame of a cowardly and trivial past, so live as not to be tortured for years, without purpose, that dying he can say, 'All my life and my strength were given to the first cause in the world — The liberation of manking."

7

GENERAL ZIA-UL-HAQ (1977-1988)

General Mohd. Zia ul Haq was born on 12 August 1924 at Jallandhar (India). His father was a teacher in the British army. He did his schooling at Shimla and B A Honours from St. Stephans College, Delhi. He joined Pak army in the commissioned rank in 1943. During the Second World War he had the opportunity to serve in Indonesia, Burma and Malaya.

After partition in 1947, Zia ul Haq opted to join the Pak army as most of the muslim military officers did so, at that time. He excelled in his career and held number of staff and command assignments in the Pak army. He rose to the rank of Lt General (as Corps Commander) at Multan in 1975. In 1976, he was directly promoted to be the Chief of Army Staff of the Pak's army, by Mr Z A Bhutto, superseding five senior generals. Since General Zia was very unassueming from Bhutto's view point and a man who was a simple and God fearing, did not pose any threat to Bhutto's regime in future, was picked up for the top appointment. But Mr Bhutto soon failed in his assessment when he was toppled by General Zia on 05 July 1977 in a bloodless coup, when there was a political chaos in the country, particularly between PPP and Pak National Alliance (PNA). General Zia enforced martial law in the country, for the third time in the brief history of Pak.

Since the March 1977 general elections were declared rigged and null and void, General Zia announced to hold fresh elections within 90 days and hand over the reign to the elected representatives. However instead of holding elections, he started accountability campaign against the politicians. He announced this to be the general view of the people and appointed various commissions of inquaries to nail a few of the powerful politicians including Mr. Bhutto.

On 16 September 1978, General Zia assuemed the office of President when Mr Fazal Ilahi retried. Since there was no Parliament in 1980, he opted for a different system of governance, called Majlis-i-Shoora, which included people from all walks of life ie - Ulemas, intellectuals, journalists and economists etc. This was a advisory body to the president in discharge of his duties. These all members were handpicked by the president himself, though the numbers was as high as 284.

In December 1984, held a refrendum in which he secured more than 95 percent votes in favour of his continuing as the President of Pak and carryon with process of islamisation in the country.

In February 1985, he held elections to fullfill his promise, but on no party basis. He then appointed Mr Mohd Khan Junejo as PM from the elected representatives of the assembly. Since he had complete control over the elected body and PM, he carried out certain amendments to the constitution before lifting the emergency from the country. Accordingly eighth amendment in the constitution was carried out in which powers of the president were increased investing all the legal powers in him.

However over a period of time the difference of opinion cropped up amongst politicians due to the president being all powerful and latter being just the puppets. Having sensed the dissension, Zia dissolved the assembly on 29 May 1988. In order to keep law and order under control, he once again announced to hold elections within 90 days which he, as was expected postponed, particularly in view of Benazir Bhutto returning to country and PPP gaining popularity. As ill luck would have it, General Zia ul Haq died in an aircrash on 17 August 1988 near Bhawalpur in Pak. He was burried in Islamabad with State honour.

His Performance

He took over on 05 July 1977 on the promise that he would return to civilian governance and hold general elections within 90 days. He told people of Pak that he had accepted the challenge as a true soldier of Islam. The strategies that he employed to keep the army in power was based in the name of return to democracy, Islam and economic well being of the country. Even in November 1977, the Pak Supreme court allowed the military rule under the term “the law of necessity” for a limited period till the elections were held. In order to abide by Supreme Court rulling he included Pak National Alliance leaders in his Cabinet just to give an impression that his rule was not military but more of a civilian in nature.

In order to divert the attention of people from Mr Z A Bhutto’s execution, General Zia promised elections in November 1979. But before the elections he outlawed all the political parties, gagged the press and made it clear to the supporting Pak National Alliance elements that he did not need their help any longer. He had the distinction of awarding whipping sentence to the journalists, if they did not abide by his instructions.

As luck would have it, Soviets entered Afganistan in December 1979, giving sudden boost to the position of Pak army in the eyes of the muslim world.

General Zia claimed that he was the man sent by God to rescue the people of Pak. He also claimed that in Islam it did not matter how a ruler emerged; he should be a faithful muslim. He condemned Western democracy and the political parties as unislamic.

On 06 February 1981, the PPP officially defunct, as were the other parties, and certain other political parties joined to form the Movement for Restoration of Democracy. Its demands were very simple ie -an end to martial law and the elections be held under the suspended constitution of 1973. Zia could manage this pressure and many leaders were sent to Jails. In February 1982, in a response to holding elections, Zia created and appointed Majlis-e-Shoora (A council of advisors), claiming that it was the pattern of Islamic law.

On 24 March 1981, he promulgated his provisional constitution order which took away fundamental rights, power of civil courts to hear appeals against the government related issues, right to form political parties and all provision of holding elections. As the Movement for Restoration of Democrary (MRD) decided to launch a disobedience movement, General Zia declared elections to be held by 23 March 1985. When MRD pressed for revival of 1973 constitution, he agreed to it but only after amending it to suit his military rule. During various speeches, he would say that elections would be held not to transfer powers, but to share it and that he would be the president and the PM would be either from Sindh or Baluchistan provinces, just to please the people of those areas.

General Zia, who seized power in July 1977, got some political reprieve due to Soviet invasion in bordering Afganistan. By providing a rationale for the continued martial law, it gave him and the army a measure of domestic legitimacy that had previously eluded them. The Soviets invasion also helped Zia to rebuild his external ties which had been in disarray. The execution of Mr Bhutto had troubled Pak's close friends China, Saudi Arabia and created wide spread criticism of the military ruler of Pak, in the West. Pak's relations with US had sunk to an all time low. Pak's covert acquisition of uranium enrichment technology had caused suspension of US economic and military aid to Pak in April 1979. But the Soviet's action in Afganistan totally changed the situation for Zia and the US-Pak relations again became very cordial. Overnight General Zia got internal palitical breathing room and an opportunity to refurbish his external ties. The US moved quickly to revitalize the moribund US-Pak security relationship. Pak also drew closer to its regional friends, found new support among the non-aligned nations and rapidily assumed a position of leadership within the Islamic world.

General Zia ul Haq Role in Afgan War

In 1979 Russian forces entered Afganistan led by Barbak Karmal. Afgan people organised themselves against this move in which Soviets suffered quite a bit in men and material. It is indeed correctly said about this country, that Afganistan can easily be invaded and occupied but it is difficult to hold and control it. General Zia stood firmly against this Soviet move, ofcourse without openly getting in confrontation with the Soviets. He openly asked for Russians withdrawal from Afganistan. US promptly responded to General Zia's call and supplied Pak with monetary help to finance the anti communist regime in Afganistan and also to equip the freedom fighters through Pak.

The freedom fighters and the Mujahideen put up a stiff resistance against the Soviet invasion of their country. US even supplied them surface to air stinger missiles. General Zia benifitted a lot with his anti communism dispositions. His policy of Islamisation of Pak got a boost since islam in the neighbourhood Afganistan was in danger from communist expansion. Pak also managed immense aid in terms of money and military equipment from US for the preparation to stop Soviets, should it manage to reach the Pak border from Afganistan. This helped Pak army update its deficient inventory and they became well equipped to thwart any external aggression.

Taliban

Since Soviet Union reached the point of disintegration they preforce agreed to the proposal of withdrawal from Afganistan. General Zia was instrumental in reaching an accord which was signed on 04 April 1988 at Geneva. Though Soviets complied with the Geneva agreement and withdrew from Afganistan, but the fighting between various clans and mujahideens continued among themselves for supremacy and power. The result was the birth of Taliban, which was favourable to Pak government. Taliban displayed strict Islamic code of conduct and zero tolerance to any other religion in the country. The drug cultivation which was main source of revenue for Afganistan was totally stopped. After 11 September 2001, world found Taliban to be the training ground and a nursery for the terrorists. The Taliban were removed by force by US led troops and now an elected government under Mr. Karzai has been installed. But the problem has not been solved. The Taliban are up again in arms and are giving a tough time to US led NATO forces in Afganistan. Pak is again active in helping Taliban secretly; openly General Musharaff is with US.

Pak top national security agency the ISI monitored the activities and provided the advice and support to the mujahideen and the commandos of the Pak SSG guided the operations inside Afganistan. In the muslim world Pak increasingly assumed a leading role. But as a price for Pak's involvement, the refugee burden caused serious trouble and a drain on Pak's economy. Soviet and Afgans carried out raids on Mujahideens in Pak territory, which became a serious cause of security concern to Pak. Credit for Soviet defeat in Afganistan is attributed mainly to mujahideen and their Pak monitors and also to the change in policy of Soviet Union not to seriously involve in foreign countries.

Execution of Mr Z A Bhutto

Shortly after taking over the country, General Zia announced that he would hold elections within 90 days. He believed that in March 1977 elections Mr Bhutto's PPP had won the elections by rigging and that since Mr Bhutto had become so unpopular, he would be defeated in the ensuing elections and as such Pak would be rescued from the Bhutto's misrule. But Zia was shocked to see that inspite of the so called misrule, the instant magic of Bhutto's appeal was still intact. Crowds flocked to Mr Bhutto, which they had seldom done in the past. Bhutto's mass appeal was pitted against military power and Zia seeing this all happen, postponed the promised elections and put Mr Bhutto behind the bars. General Zia who had tampered with the 1973 constitution by force, knew that as per the law he had committed 'High Treason' for which the panalty was 'death'. He realized that 'Alive Bhutto' could be very dangerous man and if he is let loose, he would be back in power and the first thing Bhutto would do, would be to settle scores with him. Therefore General Zia wanted to fix Bhutto once for all. He knew that it would be either his neck or that of Mr Bhutto and to save his own, the military supremo cornered Mr Bhutto.

Mr Bhutto was charged for rigging the March 1977 elections and later he was framed into a more serious charge that in a conspiracy hatched by Mr Bhutto, two members of the Federal Security (the personal Security Service created by Bhutto) tried to kill a political leader, a opponent of Mr Bhutto and ultimtely managed to kill the father of that leader.

For the trial of Mr Bhutto, two judges, who had earlier granted habeas corpus petition were excluded and instead the chief justice of Lahore High Court included himself inspite of a dispute he had with Mr Bhutto due to his supersession when Mr Bhutto was in power. This was intended to settle scores with Mr Bhutto and General Zia did approve of it. As was expected Mr Bhutto was awarded death sentence by Lahore High Court, which was later confirmed by the Supreme Court of Pak.

Some of neighbouring islamic countries requested General Zia not to execute Mr Bhutto and even some of them offered to keep Bhutto in their country for a life term. But General Zia did not agree to this proposal because he was apprehensive, that Bhutto alive anywhere would return one day to Pak, since most of those countries who offered this, were not too sure of their own thrones in their respective countries.

Mr Z A Bhutto, the elite of Pak, was hanged on 04 August 1979.

It was the game of survival of the fittest. General Zia being in power carried the day. It was rather unfortunate and undigestable by the people of Pak and the world that a man (General Zia) who was promoted out of turn to the top army post by Mr Bhutto, superseding five senior generals to him, could do so disregarding all the obligations. General Zia always paid glowing tribute to Mr Bhutto even after taking over as the Chief of Army Staff. An extract of General Zia ul Haq speech at Staff College Quetta in April 1976, at a dinner given in honour of Mr Bhutto is -

> "Those of us who are aware of the facts and figures are quite certain that the amount of attention which the Pak army received since 1971 till to date, has no parallel in the history of Pak army prior to 1971.
>
> With all this Sir, I personally and on behalf of Pak army have nothing tangible to offer as yet. All I can say is that perhaps one day, by the grace of God, while you are still present, this Pak army can show that all the attention and affection that it received from you did not go waste....
>
> I am saying this in very simple and humble words from the bottom of my heart that we thank you, Sir, for that you are doing and what you have done for us in particular."

This is one side of a military ruler, praising his master to the hilt, whether to please him or to fool him, is anyone's guess today. But whatever be the case, the execution of such an outstanding statesman of the country was not justified at all that too on very flimsy ground of abethment. General Zia having put Bhutto behind bars and having played with the clauses of 1973 constitution, which amounted to high treason, punishable by death as per the laws, probably had no alternative than to go ahead, to save his own neck. This is how Pak lost an outstanding diplomat whose contribution in nation building had been enormous.

General Zia as a Fanatic

General Zia took over as Chief Martial Law Administrator on 05 July 1977. He gave a new boost to Islamisation and used the name of Islam even to compensate for his inadquacies. Infact most of the rulers have used religion as an aid in their country (Pak), particularly so since Pak was created in the name of Islam. General Zia extensively used the name of islam to exploit the religious sentiments of masses; also it was taken help of, to undo the popularity of Mr Bhutto. He knew that people of Pak by and large were conservative and they could easily be swayed in the name of religion.

Soon on becoming the Chief Martial law Administrator, Zia announced that islamic law would be enforced in the country. Infact Pak's descent into radicalism began way back in 1949, when the constituent assembly passed a resolution, declaring Pak an Islamic State. This shocked all other minority communities in Pak. Mr. Jinnah's deputy, Liaquat Ali Khan, tabled the resolution's islamic provisions and won the vote by majority of 21 to 10. All who voted against it were Hindus. Liaquat assured Hindus that time that Islamic State did not mean that only muslims could hold high offices in politics of Pak. But 1956 Constitution later ruled that only a muslim could be the President of Pak. Infact all government of Pak took this seriously and produced one Islamic law after another. In 1974, Pak had laid restrictions on freedom of religion, when it passed a unanimous law baning members of the Ahmadiyya sect from referring to themselves as muslims. This law still exists and is supported by the Ulema.

Infact General Zia crossed all the limits and carried the weapon of religion too far in his governance of Pak. He made serious efforts to bring the legal, social, economic and political institutions of the country in conformity with the Islamic principles, values and traditions in the light of Quran and Sunnah, to enable the people of Pak to lead their lives as per the laws of Islam.

He took number of steps to remove the westernise practices which had crept in the society and employed eminent scholars of Islam to help him enforce his islamic policies. General Zia introduced the 'Zakat', 'Ushr', 'Islamic Hadood' and penal code in the country. The Zakat and Ushr ordinance to islamize the ecnomy system was introduced on 20 January 1980. It covered Islamic organisations, associations and all financing institutions. Zakat was deducted at source by the banks and Ushr was levied on the agriculture product. The taxes collected were spent on the needy. Shias were exempted from the taxes due to their difference in the religious belief about the subject.

A federal Shariah court was established to decide cases according to the teachings of Holy Quaran. Appeals against the lower and high courts were to be presented before the Shariah Court for hearing. Blesphemy was made punishable by death instead of life imprisonment. General Zia also selected Majlis-i-Shoora in 1980. It was to be the Islamic Parliament and act as the Parliament of Pak in place of national assembly. The members for the Shoora were drawn from the elites of Pak, belonging to various professional fields. The Shoora was an advisory body for the President of Pak.

Teaching of Islamic subjects and Arabic were made compulsory. The media was also brought under strict control of the Islamic law. On TV, female artists were to cover their heads. In the army the religious teachers were made as commissioned officers just to make it lucrative for the qualified people in religion, to join the army.

The sanctity of Ramazan was strictly enforced. The religious institutions became the power centre in the country. Number of new mosques were constructed. A fine upto three months imprisonment was introduced for violation of Ramazan. A program to ensure regular prayers called 'Nizam-i-Salaat' was also introduced by General Zia.

He was very strict while dealing with laws for the women. He strictly advocated the theory of 'Char Diwar' or 'Chadar' for them. He flogged women for adultary. The testimony of women in law of the land, particularly in cases of rape and adultry was not given weightage equal to the men. General Zia wanted to make

Pak the citadel of Islam so to make Pak a unique Islamic State in the Islamic world. The lack of consensus among the religious authorities combined with country wide protests forced Zia to hold back on making Shariah law the law of 'the country'.

Some of the religious laws made by General Zia, are still practised in Pak.

Conclusion

General Zia was extremely skillfull in protecting his base in the army. To ensure effective control he was concurrently the Chief of Army Staff of Pak army, Chief Martial Law Administrator and the President of Pak.

He very carefully juggled senior military appointments. The satisfaction level of the army was also augmented by an arrangement, under which Pak military service personal were seconded to the armed forces of the Persian gulf countries, where they were much better paid. Those retired from the army service, got land allotment and some were given other lucrative jobs in government or economic enterprises. Approximately ten percent of the senior posts were earmarked for the military personnel.

Provincialism increased during General Zia's tenure but he handled it very skillfully. The problem of unrest in Balochistan was handled better than his predecessor Mr Z A Bhutto. Zia used various schemes of economic development to please the Baloch. NWFP however remained quiet due to Soviet pressure next door in Afganistan. But the long festing division between Sindhis and non-Sindhis turned into voilance in Sindh. The Mujahirs formed a new organisation.

Zia's determined pursuit of non war pact with India bore some fruits in 1981. The two countries agreed to the proposal of peace and friendship treaty and established the joint commission for resolving bilateral issues. General Zia responded with sensitivity and statemanship to November 1984 assasination of Mrs Indira Gandhi and met Mr Rajiv Gandhi a number of times. However despite various visits by the head of states from both the sides, the tension between India and Pak did not normalize. The desire for a nuclear bomb, that Mr Bhutto wanted to acquire, continued by General Zia also. The dispute over demarcation of LOC and dispute over of Siachen, led to large number of local skirmishes on the border. Indian were also not happy with Zia's support to Indian Sikh extremists. At one stage, a situation was reached, when armies of both the countries had come face to face under garb of training exercises, but General managed to get over the tension and a war was averted.

General Zia also tried very hard to maintain close ties with the muslim world. He also tried to resolve war between Iraq and Iran which earned him good admiration in the muslim countries. He also fought successfully proxy war in Afganistan against the Soviets and avoided direct confrontation with them.

Zia continued on the old policy intiated by Mr Bhutto of having ties with the Middle East and sending troops to Saudi Arabia and training missions in other countries. Zia also played an important role in organising Islamic conference where a Pakistani became the general secretary of this organisation. However US was unhappy with Zia due to Mr Bhutto's execution by him and nuclear proliferation. Pak also gained an important position internationally under Zia, which was due to his supportive role in Afganistan during the Soviet invasion and soon dropped on withdrawal of Soviets from there.

8

Ms. Benazir Bhutto (1988-1990 & 1993-96)

Benazir was born on 21 June 1953 at Karachi. She is the eldest child of Late Mr Z A Bhutto. She did her initial schooling in Pak and her graduation in Political Science from Harvard University, US. After doing her post graduation she returned to Pak in June 1977. Since she was still underage to enter politics, she began assisting her father Mr Z A Bhutto. In July 1977, General Zia ul Haq took over the regime in a bloodless army coup from her father and imposed martial law. Benazir after spending nearly six and half years in jail, went into exile in England for two years. On 10 April 1986, she returned to Pak to contest assembly elections which General Zia had announced to hold. She took active part in campaigning for Movement for Restoration of Democracy. On 18-December 1987, she married Asif Ali Zardari in Karachi. She contested the elections which were held by Mr Ghulam Ishaq Khan, the acting

President of Pak, after the death of General Zia in an air crash.

Benazir sought a rulling from the Supreme Court of Pak to allow elections on the political party basis, which was conceded. She then contested the election and her party PPP won 97 out of 207 seats in the national assembly. She became the Prime Minister of Pak on 02 December 1988, with the help of 21 members of Tribal areas and MQM. Mr Ghulam Ishaq Khan was appointed as the President of Pak.

She became the youngest PM at the age of 35 years and the first women to be PM in the Islamic Countries. She lifted ban on student trade unions, which was imposed during the martial law regime of General Zia ul Haq and also hosted the fourth SAARC summit in December 1988 in Islamabad. Due to difference of opinion on certain ideologies, she was dismissed by the President under his constitutional powers, on 06 August 1990. But she soon returned to power in october 1993 elections, her party (PPP) winning the largest number of seats ie 86. But she was again dismissed on corruption charges by Mr Ahmed Khan Leghari in November 1996, who was the President of Pak, though nominated by her party PPP and her government.

She has been the political activist with PPP from 1977 onwards. She has been repeatedly imprisoned and kept under house arrest by the Pak government and a political exile in London.

She became the PM after winning the elections in 1988, but her government was illigally dismissed by the President in 1990. She again came to power in 1993, but was again removed by the President in 1996 on various corruption charges. Since then She and PPP have been subjected to political presecution first by Nawaj Shariff government and then by General Musharaff's regime. She has been facing all the coercion and intimidation with courage and her party PPP is still a force to be reckoned with in Pak, even under the military ruler, General Musharaff.

With Benazir in power, relations between India and Pak became more tense. Bhutto openly supported the muslim rebels in J&K, who were involved in the act of terrorism and spordic fighting with the Indian army. She also announced that Pak would continue with its nuclear weapons development program, raising concerns that a nuclear arms race could start between Pak and India, which is believed to have had nuclear technology since 1970s. In February 1992, Pak government admitted to having nuclear capabilities and claimed that its nuclear weapons programme had been stopped at a level achieved in 1989, that is with an actual uclear device far from completion. In 1996, the US stopped the supply of military weapons to Pak owing to China having supplied nuclear weapons related material in 1995. Relations between India and Pak detriorated in early 1996, when each country accused the other of conducting nuclear tests.

Pak generally has been considered a moderate Islamic State, except for the period under General Zia ul Haq, Islamic fundamentalist began gaining influence in 1990s. There were persistant reports of discrimination against religious minorities. In June 1995 voilance flared up in Karachi over Bhutto's alleged condemnation of the ethnically Mohajir Qaumi Movement, leaving nearly 300 dead.

In October 1995, a number of army officers were arrested over an attempted Islamic fundamentalist coup. Tension with India following a mysterious rocket strike on a mosque in pak province of Azad Kashmir, bordering India, escalated in heavy fighting along the Kashmir ceasefire line in January 1996.

Inquiries against corruption allegations against Bhutto family began soon after Mr Nawaj Shariff came into power. Major cases were filed with Pak's accountability commission in January 1998. Although the family's Swiss Bank accounts had been frozen in September but courts in the UK questioned the move and did not cooperate with the Pak government concerning Bhutto's accounts in that country. Bhutto in still out of Pak for the fear of arrest by the military regime on the charges of corruption, which are still pending against her in Pak courts.

Benazir was the first woman PM of a muslim state. She benifitted by her family background to reach to that position in that young age. She inherited her father Mr Z A Bhutto's party (PPP), which had won the elections, but she was not in position to muster enough strength to bring in changes in the constitution, which could strengthen her position. She also faced problems in dealing with the army, their involvement in the politics of the country, the role of Islam and a few ethnic problems. Benazir assumption of Pak's regime brought lot of hope to the people of Pak. She was able to introduce a number of welfare projects, like increase in provincial autonomy, improvement in education, introduction of comprehensive health policy, enhanced rights of women with equal pay for equal work. But she could not deal with the hardcore representatives of the government and failed to translate her policies into action. The country's sense of disillusionment increased as she failed to full fill her promises, relating to improvement in economy, employment and other development programs. She also could not control the drug mafia in the country, which was running a parallel economy.

She faced another challenge, that was her family fued which badly appeared in the Pak press. The fued pitted her against her brother Murtaza and mother Nusrat, over dynastic control of PPP. Though her brother could not damage the position of Benazir, particularly so since he himself was jailed for long outstanding chargs of terrorism, when returned from Damascus. She also expelled her mother from the chairperson of PPP for her role in support of her son in political ambitions.

9

Mr. Nawaz Shariff

(Nov 1990 - Oct 1993 & Feb 1997 - Oct 1999)

He was born in Lahore on 25 December 1949 in the family of an industrialist. He after his initial education, did his law from Punjab University in Pak. He first became the finance minister in 1981 in the Punjab state government. In 1985 general elections, Nawaj Shariff won with an overwhelming majority, both in National and Provincial assemblies. On 09 April 1991 he became the chief Minister of Punjab and again in the elections of 1998, he came back as the chief Minister of Punjab again.

On 06 November 1990, Nawaj Shariff was sworn in as the PM of Pak after he won general elections in October 1990. But he could not complete the tenure of PM and was dismissed by the President in April 1993. However with the help of Supreme Court of Pak, he regained his post of PM, but had to resign again in July 1993, alongwith the President of Pak. However in February 1997 he was reelected PM of Pak with an overwhelming majority.

During his tenure as the PM, efforts were made to improve the lot of industries including private sectors. His most important contribution was economic growth, despite US embargo and sanctions on Pak. Taking advantage of his absolute majority in the national assembly, he repealed the eighth amendment in the Constitution of Pak, which withdrew the powers of the President to dissolve elected governments at will. He added another clause in the Constitution bringing in anti-defection bill. These added a landmark in the Constitutional history of Pak.

During his tenure, relations of Pak with the Central Asian Muslim republics were strengthened.

Nawaj Shariff faced a serious confrontation with the Judiciary and the executives, which eventually led to the resignation of President Leghari, on 02 December 1997. He carried out useful amendments in the Constitution of Pak but the fifteenth amendment was seen by the people as an effort to acquire additional powers for himself. Soon a conflict came up between him and the military generals. The confrontation led to the resignation of General Jahangir Karamat and on 07 October 1998, General Musharaff was promoted in place of General Karamat, the Chief of Pak army.

It was during his tenure that Pak carried out its nuclear tests on 28 May 1998, in response to Indian detonation of its five nuclear devices. He also proclaimed an emergency on 28 May 1998, the day these nuclear tests were carried out. All fundamental rights were suspended and all foreign currency accounts in Pak banks were frozen.

On 12 October 1999, Mr. Nawaj Shariff was overthrown in a bloodless military coup by General Pervez Musharaff, the Chief of Pak army. Controversy over the Kargil operations, corruption charges and plane conspiracy case, were considered to be the main reasons for his removal. As per the report by Lal Khan, Editor of Jeddo Judh of 19 October 1999, a Pak Airline (PIA) carrying General Musharaff back home from Colmbo on 12 October, was refused permission to land at Karachi airport. The plane hovered at Karachi airport for 48 minutes and the pilot was instructed to take the flight to Dubai or India, by Mr Nawaj Shariff. The pilot reported that he was left fuel only for six minutes. He was then asked to land at some airport in Sindh, from where Musharaff could be arrested with ease. General Musharaff took control of communication system and ordered his officers to launch a counter operation as per the plan which had been prepared in advance. In the meantime Mr Shariff had already announced dismissal of General Musharaff and nomination of General Ziaudin Ahmed the ISI Chief as the Pak army Chief in place of Musharaff. The rival factions of the army came very close to an armed conflict which though was averted at the last minute. In the meantime pro-Musharaff troops stormed Karachi airport building and rescued General Musharaff's family who had been in police captivity for a few hours. Thereafter Mr Nawaj Shariff was taken into military custody.

After military take over, Nawaj Shariff, his brother and five other officials were booked on charges of hijacking, kidnapping and attempted murder in the plane conspiracy. The prosecution case was based on a police report filed by an army Colonel. Nawaj Shariff, in his capacity as PM, was accused of giving orders to the Civil Aviation Authorities of Pak to prevent a Colambo-Karachi Pak international Airliner, with General Musharaff on board, from landing at Karachi or anywhere else in Pak. He was tried for attempted murder in 'Plane Conspiracy' case in an anti terrorist court in Karachi. Mr. Nawaj Shariff was found guilty of the charge and sentenced to life imprisonment. Fearing similar fate as that of late Mr Z A Bhutto in the hands of a military ruler, the Saudi Arabia Royal family managed to get Mr Nawaz Shariff out of Pak and he is presently in exile in Saudi Arabia, with his close family.

Mr Nawaz Shariff was convinced that solution to Pak's political problems was free market reforms and economic growth and he thus liberalized foreign exchange regulations and denationalized public sector industrial enterprises and financial institutions. A number of important industries such as electricity generation, shipping, airlines, highway construction and a few others were opened to private sector except arms manufacturing industries; which needed government permission. However some of the opposition parties were not in favour of such a liberalisation.

Even during Mr Shariff's regime, lawlessness in tribal provinces of Sindh took alarming proportion. The tribals outgunned the police because of sophisticated weapons they got from the neighbouring Afganistan.

10

General Pervez Musharaff

(Oct 1999 - Till Date)

He was born in Delhi on 11 August 1943. After partition his parents migrated to Karachi. He belongs to a middle class family background. He had his initial education in Pak and did college in Lahore. He then joined the Pak army as commissioned officer in 1964 in the Artillery. He took active part in 1965 and 1971 Indo-Pak wars. He is graduates from command and Staff College Quetta, and did RCDS (Royal College of Defence Studies) from U.K. He got maried in 1968 and has a happy family.

He was promoted to the rank of General and was appointed COAS of Pak on 07 October 1998 by Nawaj Shariff, superseding five senior generals. He replaced General Jahangir Karamat who resigned due to difference of opinion with the govt. General Musharaff took over the reigns of the country on 12 October 1999 in a bloodless coup and became the Chief Executive.

Later he became the President of Pak on 20 June 2001 and thereafter in a refrendum he legalized his appointment as the President of Pak for five years on 30 April 2002. In accordance with a deal with political parties he agreed to leave the appointment of President on 31 December 2004, but he has again manipulated yet another term of president for the next five years by amending the Constitution and gaining the vote of confidence from the Parliament and provincial assemblies.

The military take over on 12 October 1999 by General Musharaff was as usual attributed to help the country get over the turmoil and uncertainty. Supreme Court of Pakistan also accepted this plea that the move by the army to take over was for a noble cause. Supreme Court further ruled that there was no other way to deal with the Corrupt politicians, civil servants and others except the army take over under the prevailing circumstances, created by Mr. Shariffs corrupt govt. The Supreme Court also directed that the elections be held within three years in Pak to restore democratic govt.

General Pervez Musharaff took over as President of Pak on 20 June 2001, by removing Mr Rafiq Tarar before he completed his five years tenure as President of Pak. Soon on taking over he dissolved all democratic bodies and claimed that his take over was based on constitutional, political and economic reasons and he promised to fullfill the aspirations of his countrymen. As the stars favoured the uniformed President the 9/11 terrorist action in US occured and US leaned heavily on Pak support to eliminate the root of the trouble once for all. The Taliban were on the rampage and there too General Musharaff's help became very crucial for the US to conduct antiterrorism campaign.

Thus General Musharaff became a nodal agency on the international scene in combating terrorism. He very openly supported actions against Taliban and after the Taliban were ousted he offered all possible help to new elected government of Afganistan.

President Musharaff held elections in Oct 2002 as per the direction of SC and his promise to the people of Pak. As per the election results National Assembly and Senate came back into existance and Mr. Z K Jamali became the PM. The General relinguished the appointment of Chief Executive, however he continues to be COAS in addition to be the President of Pak. The newly elected Parliament did not agree to the status of the President who had the powers to dissolve the National Assembly at will and as such the Parliament was non functional for a year or so. Seeing the pressure building and also to break the deadlock, General Musharaff agreed to relinguish the appointment of COAS on 31 December 2004 and aso gave up some powers which he assumed soon on taking over the reigns of Pak. However he continued to retain both the jobs ie President and COAS.

General Musharaff sought vote of confidence under the constitutional provisions of seventh and passed by two third majority of the Parliament, allowing him full term as President till 2007. In order to bring in controlled democracy, President Musharaff introduced local govt system on the similar lines as was done by Ayub Khan during his regime. Elections to local bodies were conducted. In order to ensure max participation the voting age was lowered from 21 to 18 years and one third of the total seats, were reserved for the women candidates. This was basically designed to transfer power from top echelon of the system to the grassroot level. The local bodies were made accountable to the people which ensure speedy desposal of cases.

Some of the Important Events

Kargil War 1999

In February 1999 Mr. Vajpayee, Indian Prime Minister made a historic bus ride to sign a declaration in Lahore with Mr. Nawaj Shariff, Prime Minister of Pak. General Pervez Musharaff who was the Chief of Pak Army delibrately kept away from Lahore sending a strong message that Pak army does not approve of the agreement being signed. The declaration contained the following important aspect which were part of confidence building measures between the two countries.

(a) Intensify their efforts to resolve all issue including issue of J&K.

(b) Refrain from intervention and interference in other's internal affairs.

(c) Intensify their composite dialogue process for an early and positive outcome of the agreed bilateral agenda.

(d) Take immediate steps for reducing the risk of accidental or unauthorised use of nuclear weapons and discuss concepts and doctrines with a view to elaborating measures for confidence building in the nuclear and conventional fields, aimed at prevention of conflict.

(e) Reafferm their commitment to the goals and objectives of SAARC and concentrate their efforts towards the realization of the SAARC vision for the year 2000 and beyond with a view of promoting the welfare of people of South Asia and improve quality of life through accelerated economic growth, social progress and cultural development.

(f) Reafferm their condemnation of terrorism in all its forum and menifestations and their determination to combat this menace.

(g) Promote and protect all human rights and fundamental freedom.

When there were ongoing peace dialogue between the two countries, Pak army surreptitiously crossed the LOC and occupied dominating hights in Kargil Sector. Indian army was caught unaware by that move since they always considered this area impregnable. These were Kashmir Mujahideens supported by Pak army regulars who made such a daring thrust with a view to have dealt India in its most stunning blow in Kashmir since 1948. Pak could have severed Leh from Srinagar, trapped the Indian forces on Siachen glacier, questioned the sanctity of the entire LOC, raised banner of militant revolt in the valley and made its perennial fantasy of internationalize the Kashmir dispute.

Unfortunately for the Pak army, within just eight weeks of war, Pak found its decisions an audicious gamble beginning to go away and Mr. Shariff alongwith his foreign minister dashed to US on 04 July 99 to seek a wayout of noose which was tightening around Pak's neck in Kargil.

Indian army evicted the Pak troops from the vital hights from where they threatened strategic Srinagar-Leh highway and thwarted the Pak objectives of isolating Ladakh from Kashmir valley. By following a policy of restraint and not crossing the LOC, Indian govt also won diplomatic war with Pak's close allies like China and US. As a matter of fact, US in strong words asked Pak to pull back its troops and used its clouts to get G-8 countries to endorse much the same message, despite stiff resistence from Japan and Canada.

Kargil war brought a fierce patriotic upsurg throughout India. Solidarity with 'Soldier' apart it renewed expression of people's faith in India. The war did not only generate patriotic fervency, it gave the Indian 'Soldier' a new respect in the society. Kargil war adequately demonstrated the alertness and sensitivity of the proud and eager Indian army. It also indicated that military thinking had become predominant in the reaction to such Pak moves and that India would not be under restrained by political considerations.

General Musharaff's absence from Lahore on the day of signing of the peace proposal between the two elected heads of the countries was attributed to his being busy in infiltrating the Pak troops and irregulars across the LOC in Kargil. The Pak govt. repeatedly made attempts to make it appear to the international press that the intrusion were really the work of indigenous Kashmiris, but the propaganda failed miserably. The Kargil war in India left bitter memories of the peace process betrayed. This marked General Musharaff in the eyes of most Indian policy makers as a man unworthy of trust.

Agra Summit

There was a meeting in Agra from 14 to 16 July 2001, between General Pervez Musharaff and Mr Atal Behari Vajpayee, Prime Minister of India to resolve various outstanding issues between the two countries. The meeting began with a high hope from both the sides. The meeting was held in a very cordial atmosphere and lasted a long session of discussions each day. The important issues discussed included Kashmir, cross border terrorism, nuclear risk reduction, release of

POWs and allied subjects. General Musharaff was also afforded an opportunity by the Indian govt to meet the representations of Kashmir Hurriyat Conference. Despite the best efforts from both the sides no agreement could be reached. However both sides agreed to burry the past and continue the efforts for normalization.

9/11 Attack on US-World Trade Centre

After the terrorist attack on 11 September 2001 on the World Trade Centre in US, the President of US decided to go all out to punish the prepetrators of such an act which left the entire world shocked for the moment. The fingers ultimately pointed towards Osama Bin Laden and the Taliban for the attack. Since US needed close support in terms of providing bases and control over inter border movement of Taliban terrorists from Pak, the country shot-into limelight and General Musharaff became very important to US. However General Musharaff was apprehensive of acting against a muslim country and as such expected backlash from internal militants and religious groups and organisations. He however managed to convince some political leaders about the benefits of such a help to US at that juncture, though conservatives still opposed this move. It was very difficult decision on part of Pak to offer open help particularly to use of its soil by US to attack Taliban in Afganistan who were a close partner during Soviet invasion to push the Soviets out of

Afganistan. Under pressure from US, General Musharaff agreed to help the US coalition forces to deal with Taliban.

The attack on Taliban bases began after a month of 11 September 2001 attack on World Trade Centre in US. The US and colition partners carried out extensive aerial bombardment of Afganistan that led to killing of large number of Talibans. Ultimately Taliban regime was toppled and a caretaker govt. was installed to run the country.

There was again an influx of refugees from Afganistan into Pak. Osama Bin Laden still remains out of the reach of US, but their operations in Afganistan continue.

General Election of 2002

On 10 October 2002, General Election as were promised by General Musharaff was held. Major political parties of the country participated. The national and provincial elections were held on the same day. The voting booths for women voters were seggregated. The elections were observed by a large number of international observers; including European Union and Commonwealth countries. Many people could not contest the elections because they were not graduates which was made a mandatory qualification in these elections. Even people who were convicted were barred from taking part in the elections under Representation of People's Act. Ms Benazir Bhutto and Mr Nawaj Shariff were also barred from contesting these elections.

The results of these elections, however were against the prediction and assessment in which Muttaheda Majlis-e-Amal (MMA), a religious alliance secured a large number of seats emerging at the third position in the National Assembly elections. This made the opposition by the religious group, strong who always opposed Pak assisting US in dealing with Taliban. The MMA got a clear cut majority in NWFP and Baluchistan provinces and formed their own state governments. Even in other states of Pak, coalition govt were formed as none of the political parties emerged with adequate majority seats. Though the elections by and large were well conducted, yet some of the political parties alleged rigging. As no party won enough seats in the Parliament a coalition govt. was formed with Mr. Zafarullah Khan Jamali as the Coalition Prime Minister.

Seventeenth amendment was brought in the constitution which allowed General Musharaff to continue his tenure as President of Pak till 2007 and it conferred all the powers on him even to dissolve the elected govt. and remove the PM. General Musharaff brought in number of articles in the amendment even to the effect that Chief of Pak Army is not barred from becoming the President. This also provided indemnity to all the actions of the President. In order to please the judiciary, the age of retirement for the Supreme Court Judges was increased to 65.

By early 2004, Pak seemed on the verge of political distablization. Islamic redicals were seeking to overthrow Musharaff's regime. General Musharaff opted to support US out of compulsions more for the self than the country, much against the wishes of fundamentalists in Pak. He has also assured US to help them nab Osama Bin Laden and other Al Quada leaders who are said to be hiding in Northern Pak. He is rulling a country where majority population hates US; the army rule under General Musharaff is the only hinderence for them for supporting Cause of Taliban in Afganistan.

Pak has a long history of army rule since independence. General Musharaff took over on 12 october 1999. People who were fed up of Nawaj Shariff's regime thought that the army would bring in sweeping changes to Pak by restoring the country's international image, eliminating wide spread corruption, stablizing the security situation and providing jobs and economic development. But with General Musharaff's rule, the people's hopes with the army have also waned.

The country's major politicians former PM, Benazir Bhutto and Nawaj Shariff are in exile, latter in the Middle East. Though Bhutto's Peoples Party and Shariff's Muslim League are preparing to contest elections whenever held, with the hope to draw public support for the exiled leaders. Now only the time will tell if Pak masses can rid of military rule once again in the next elections. General Musharaff will contest elections for another five years term possibly in November 2007.

The election dates will be decided by the Election Commission of Pak and General Musharaff is likely to be a candidate of PML and allies as told by Mr Durrani, Information Minister of Pak. The elections are likely to be held between 16 September to 16 October 2007. He also clarified that there is no bar for a candidate to become President for as many times. He also told that no country can force another country that its President can not be the Chief of Army Staff and that he can not wear uniform, while being President also in addition. The leader of the upper house Mr Waseem Sajjad said that assemblies would not be dissolved for the sake of Presidential elections since as per the Pak constitution the President has to be elected by a new assembly. Though the opposition is still pressing for the line of argument for the Presidential elections that the state assemblies should be dissolved and then be reelected.

General Musharaff feels that next elections will be very important as the people will reject religious extremists and bring forth the moderate leadership in Pak. He even warned the public that if the extremists win the next elections, it would be a threat to the integrity of Pak.

With economic reforms undertaken during his regime, have yeilded some results, social reform programme appear to have met with some resistance.

Musharaff's power is threatened by the extremists who have grown in strength since 11 September 2001 attack on US World Trade Centre and who are particularly angered by Musharaff's close political and military alliance with US including his support to invasion of Afganistan and his liberal views on reforming Islam. General Musharaff has servived assassination attempts by terrorists groups believed to be part of Al-Qaeda. In two instances the terrorists had inside information from a member of his military security details.

General Musharaff sent thousands of troops into the region of Wazirstan in 2002 to hunt for Osama Bin Laden and other Al Qaeda fugitives. In March 2004 heavy fighting broke out between Pak army and the militants. It was speculated that estimated 400 militants were holed up in several fortified settlements including Bin Laden's deputy, Ayman-al-Zawahiri. Clashes erupted between Pak troops who are frequently assisted by US precision stakes and Al Qaeda militants joined by Taliban forces. The struggle in Waziristan is seen as part of war on terrorism and is connected to Taliban insurgency in Afganistan. The stakes are high there and approximately one lac troops are involved in the fighting; unfortunately no news is coming from there since journalists are not safe in that area due to threat from Taliban.

Maulana Fazlur Rehman of MMA and the leader of opposition in the Pak assembly has criticized General

Musharaff's policies. He believes that these are religious groups who can maintain peace in the tribal region bodering Afganistan which is a hot bed of Taliban. Mr Rehman told that General Musharaff should avoid alienating the Taliban leaders and further accused him of misleading his allies in war against terror.

Robert Gates, Defence Secretary US has also shown his concern over negligence to the border incursions on the part of the Pak and agreed to the border security problems as they have hard evidence to this effect.

In order to gave US confidence, Pak was carrying out some operations in Afganistan. Pak military has claimed to destroy a Madarasa in October 06 in Bagur Tribal area near Afgan border. They claimed that the Madrasa was actually being used to train militants. The Pak army used helicopter gunships during the operation. The madrasa was being run by a local cleric Maulvi Liaquat who was accused of hiding local and foreign militants. He was reported killed in action. Two days before the operation, thousands of tribal militants had organised a protest rally against US and its supportive Pak administration. Some newspapers reported killing of some children in the operation but the Pak army denied it and confirmed that the operation was against approximately 80 hardcore militants hiding there. There were also reports by NATO forces that Taliban was using Afgan children as human shield against attack on them.

Comments on General Pervez Musharaff by Various Agencies

1. *Vijay Mohan- Quoting an Intelligence Assessment*

"Behind the name is a personality known to be a professionally bred morally upright soldier with strong links with fundamentalists who at times can be rash and dangerous. A well trained officer with a wide ranging mind, hardworking and appears to be thoughtful and shrewd in assessing future developments. To the outside world General Musharaff's expression appears stern and manner often abrupt. He is hot headed and is considered to be unpopular among his subordinates. He can be rash and dangerous if he feels the situation is getting out of control. He does not mix freely with officers, but prefers to interact with JCOs and other ranks. A strong personality who came to be known of his capability for taking definite decision as well as tremendous drive and tenacity. He meteoric rise in the Pak army is attributed to his professional competence and his being 'Mohajir'........

2. *B Raman (General Pervez Musharaff – His Past and Present)*

The interviews and speeches of General Musharaff since October 1998 show his thinking to be as follows:-

"The acquisition of Kashmir by Pak can wait. What is more important is to keep the Indian army bleeding in Kashmir just as the Afgan Mujahideen kept Soviet troops bleeding in Afganistan. Even if Kashmir issue is resolved, there can not be normal relations between India and Pak because Pak by frustrating India's ambitions of emerging as a major Asian power on par with China and Japan would continue to be a thorn on India's flesh. And so long as it does so, Pak would continue to enjoy the backing of China and Japan".

Musharaff's Moderate Outlook

He took over from Nawaj Shariff in a bloodless military coup, but he has promised a moderate Islamic regime. Islamists who are on rise in Pak are under reasonable control of the mil ruler. The radicalisation of Pak has happened under democrats from Liaquat to Shariff. The only other military ruler in Pak who Islamised Society further was Zia ul Haq who passed the Hudood, Qisas and Diyat Laws. Under one of them, a man may get away with killing his wife if her family accepts blood money or pardon. In another, women who were raped and could not prove that they were raped would be charged and punished for adultery. This law was overturned by General Musharaff in face of opposition from conservative muslims and Ulemas. Earlier General Musharaff withdrew from attempting to reform, blesphemi law since he did not get adequate support from the political parties. In December 1999 the Supreme Court of Pak abolished interest under

Islamic provision called 'riba' General Musharaff had to rig the court and get rid of its hardline judges. In 2006, General Musharaff stopped Lahore High Court from banning kite flying because it was unislamic. Today kite flying is permitted though only for two weeks, with a licence from the State govt. There is a reasonably good understanding between India and Pak on Kashmir, which is largely attributed to flexibility on part of Musharaff. With the opening of Srinagar-Muzzaffrabad highway, people to people contact between two countries has increased.

Islamic terror is a global threat and needs joint management by all the countries of the world. The militant groups like Lushkar-e-Taiba, Hizb-ul-Mujahideen, Jaish-e-Mohammad and others pose an equal threat to Pak leadership and General Musharaff has faced three attacks including suicide bombing that nearly took him on. His enemies today are the same extremists that Pak army nurtured first against the Soviets and now against India. They are angry with General Musharaff because of his liberal attitude and helping the US in attacking Taliban in Afganistan.

11

Pak - Sino Relations

Pak began seeking help to build up its armed forces from almost the time if became independent and by mid 1950s had become an important member of various military alliances with West Powers. These alliances included Central Treaty Organisation (CENTO) and South East Asia Treaty Organisation (SEATO). As a result Pak began to receive a major military help in terms of arms and equipment with the aim of containing spread of communism. However repeated arms embargos by US and Indian fast progress in indigenisation and self reliance on production of military hardware, Pak turned towards China for help. Pak began to build defence ties with China as part of its efforts to diversify its resources of weapons supplies and indigenise production of its defence related equipment. This friendship was later strengthened by Sino-Indian war of 1962 and Indo-Pak war of 1965, following which Beijing began to visualize Pak as its major ally in dealing with India.

China's support for Pak has helped them to play an important role in Asia more than its indegenous capabilities. US support to Pak in 1950s, later in 1980, and also as consequence of the Soviet intervention in Afganistan coupled with Chinese continuous military aid, made Pak think of nuclear umbrella to counter India's threat. Though US stopped its assistance to Pak military build up particularly those relating to Afganistan. US also opposed Pak's efforts to develop nuclear weapons and also to acquire long range missiles. The growth of extremists influence in Pak and freedom with which several powerful, fanatical and heavily armed 'Jehadi' organisations operate in that country is the cause of concern to all its neighbours, particularly India.

China's continued cooperation has greatly contributed towards building up Pak defence capabilities, thus enhancing the influence and role of the military in Pak's politics. China and Pak were generally secretive about their defence cooperation agreements and only made these public at a convinient time. This was particularly the case in regard to collaboration in Pak's nuclear and missile programme. The details of such agreement are not available, but it is guessed that Pak's nuclear programme has been only partly indigenous and China has had the foremost role in creating Pak's nuclear capabilities. Pak's strategic thinking has been mainly determined by its military, diplomatic and political rivalry with India. Pak's decision makers were aware of the continued development by India of nuclear technology and Chinese nuclear test in 1964; which they thought India would try to match. General Ayub Khan tried to explore the possibility of co-operation in 1960s in nuclear technology with China, but did not make much headway since China was trying to keep its own nuclear programme secret.

China temporarily suspended its nuclear assistance to Pak after execution of Mr Z A Bhutto and take over by General Zia ul Haq. It was revived soon after Soviet intervention in Afganistan when Pak played the role in the supply of weapons to Afganistan Mujahideens. China and Pak were worried about the Soviet Union expanding its influence into Southern Asia and China saw nothing wrong with reviving nuclear cooperation with General Zia.

China has formally become segnatory to Non-Proliferation Treaty (NPT) which places severe restraints on its nuclear collaboration with Pak. However going by the reports on transper of ring magnets, China seems to be using these non-proliferation regimes as cover while continuing its nuclear dealings with its strategic partner Pak. There is also a view that China may have already supplied enough material components and blue prints to Pak to ensure that its nuclear weapons establishment can now operate independently. The extent of Sino-Pak collaboration became clear following Pak's nuclear tests to which Chinese reaction was muted in comparision to tests by India.

China's contribution has been considerable and consistant in helping Pak in defence production. Following the US arms embargo after 1965 India-Pak war, China supplied all military hardwares and arms to Pak. These were provided without any cost until 1980 or without any condition or political strings. China's help in setting up defence industries in Pak and making it self reliant in some critical and strategic material has been immense.

After 1965 Indo-Pak war, China felt obliged to make some non-committal gestures at the last minute to compensate for the fact that despite China's apparent pledges of support to Pak during war, she had been conspicuously inactive. Except making some propaganda, Chinese had done nothing significant, of course pinning down Indian forces deployed on Sino-Indian border. Chinese raised issue of Sikkim again. This threat created headlines and raised appropriate caution on Indian side at no cost to Chinese. Chinese sent formal note to India accusing her of voilating Sikkim border several times. The statement contended that India had continued to intrude on the Chinese territory since 1962 and that Indian aggression against any of its neighbours concerns all the neighbours. The possibility and threat of Chinese involvement was used extensively by Pak leaders. The signing of Sino-Pak border protocal and cultural pact in Rawalpindi on 27 March 1965, was turned into major propaganda event by the Pak media.

Since Pak established diplomatic relations with China, it has always remained cordial and trouble free. There was only one issue, the demarcation of border between Pak and China which could have led to some sort of confrontation, but the issue was resolved by the two, amicably through negotiation in 1963. Actually Pak's friendship with China has been at two levels, one at political elite's level and second at the military level; latter being so since Pak has been ruled most of the times by military rulers.

Pak strategic location affords it an opportunity to disturb Chinese main bases at Kashgar and Sinkiang, the centre of all troops and logistic moving Southward, from Gilgit airfield. This in theory, the power controlling Gilgit could seriously threaten Chinese Southward expansionist plans against Indian sub continent, at least until a more remote Sinkiang base and an alternative communication artery could be developed. The Karakoram road was one in the offing.

The Karakoram highway has been the focus of military and strategic analysts. It was a pioneering venture of Pak during 1959 when work was started on it that time known as 'Indus valley road'. After 1965 war, Pak concluded an agreement to extend the road to Chinese border. In 1967, it was decided to transform the road into an all weather and dual carriage highway over the Karakoram pass. The road was completed by both the countries in 1978. The highway starts at Havelian, 90 Km North of Islamabad and propels itself through Abbotabad, Mansehra, Thakot, Chilas, Gilgit, Hunza Valley and crosses the Karakoram range through 16000 ft Khunjerab pass into the Chinese province of Xinjiang. This has become an important life line between Pak and China and has helped in the economic and social emancipation of hither to backward regions.

Chinese change in her foreign policy while dealing with Indo-Pak matters has now undergone slight change which is due to emphasis its leaders have given to its economic development. Also Chinese reluctance to openly support Pak during Kargil operation has also to do something with the ups and downs in Sino-US relationship. China probably does not want hostile Indian while it is in confrontation with US and issues like Taiwan. Chinese leadership have also realized India's economic potential and politico-military dimensions.

Sino-Pak relations have long thrived on military and strategic cooperation. Over a time, this cooperation has tremendously helped Pak economically and militarily in which military and strategic interests still dominate their relations. Pak on the other hand is creating a tax free 'Exclusive Industrial Zone' to help Chinese investment in Pak. The Chinese products have flooded Pak much to the dislikes of Pak manufacturers. China at the same time is pursuing active diplomacy to engage Pak leadership to keep its strategic interest alive. Over the past two years there has been a dramatic increase in bilateral trade between China and Pak. China has become Pak's largest trading partner in Asia, surpassing even Japan. Dispite efforts at Public diplomacy, it is China's ever growing strategic interest with Pak that overrides all other concerns.

It is said that younger generation in Pak is not satisfied with the Sino-Pak relations. For decades this relationship has been the exclusive domain of senior political leadership on both the sides. The younger lot on both sides have had more exposure to western education. The younger Chinese intellectuals and policy analysts mostly educated in US, carry some perceptions and biases against Pak, an Islamic state. The fears about Islam and clashes between Islam fundamentalists and non-islamic countries dominate their thinking. The new generation of Chinese intellectuals is more susceptable to global perceptions. It finds a socially liberal India more attractive than Pakistan's image of a socially-stunted and politically unstable state.

Pak is also getting restless with the improving relations between India and China. The way Sino-Indian trade is booming is certainly a cause of concern to Pak leadership. They feel intensifying trade and commerce would naturally raise the stakes for China in its relationship with India and China will have to bring in changes in its foreign policy towards the Indian sub continent. China has already shown change of her position on issues concerning India. They refused to back

Pak's attack in Kargil in 1999. Pak leadership feels any gain for India in its ties with China, must be a loss for Pak. India also fully understands that Chinese interest in India is purely economic based where as with Pak it is strategic requirement for China to maintain balance of power in South Asia and then make an endeavour to emerge as a world power. The later is far more important in overall aims of China. Besides, India has legitimate grievances about the past nuclear and missile cooperation between China and Pak, which has created a serious security problem for the Indians.

Though China does not hold same views on terrorism as India, but they are also highly concerned with it. The attack on 11 September 2001 on US World Trade Centre has shaken everyone. The concerns about Pak becoming an epicentre of religious extremism and international terrorism are not limited to India alone. During General Musharaff's visit to Beijing, he was under certain pressure to give assurances that Pak will not allow its soil to be used by muslim separatists. There have been reports about links between China's Xinjiang province and terrorists outfit in Pak.

China casts a long and ominous shadow over all of Asia. It is a nation with very large population. Their territory is generally self sufficient in most of the natural resources and once exploited fully, China can become a world power. It occupies a strategic position in Asia. From its central position it can threaten Japan, Korea in the East, the Peninsula of South East Asia, the Sub continent of India and Pakistan over its Himalayan border in the South and Soviet Asia in the North. There is a race between two communist powers ie Russia and China as to who should lead the Communist world.

China's elusive strategic equation with Pak poses a hindrance to any substantive improvement in India's relations with China. China has been the biggest supplier of military hardware to Pak, some of which are being made available to Kashmiri militants also. The core of Sino-Pak ties comprises the transfer of military hardward and technology besides nuclear cooperation. While China may make sugar coated friendly statements, the litmus test of her real intentions need to be gauged from the nature of her relationship with Pak. Islamabad has been getting weapons at subsidised rates from China. Pak and China entered into cooperation of battle tank code named Main Battle Tank 2000. The Chinese largesse so far includes about 1700 tanks, 400 fighter aircrafts and 30 naval ships. The Chinese have also established a tank factory in Pak for production of a modern tank with 105 mm gun at the rate of 200 tanks a year. Assistance has also been provided to develop the Pakistani version of Hy5 missiles, similar to the American stinger, as also Red Arrow-8 anti tank missile.

China has also established cordial political relations with many other countries in the Indian ocean region especially Myanmar, Sri Lanka, Bangladesh and

Pakistan. Thus apart from enhancing its economy through better trade relations, China has also emerged a prime supplier of arms to the security forces of these countries. The spadework that China has been doing for some years now, is likely to pay dividents when China decides to make its naval presence felt in the Indian ocean region. A Chinese military presence in the Indian ocean will directly pose threat to India's security. The threat will be political and military if Pak and Bangladesh agree to provide some port facilities to Chinese navy. The political tilt of some of our neighbouring countries towards Beijing under such a situation will grow and become stronger alongwith the growth of the Chinese military capabilities. In the event of armed conflict between India and Pak, the presence of Chinese navy in the Indian ocean will certainly work against the interest of India. Though China and Pak would be too happy to create such a situation for India's security, but, Chinese navy at present has still not overcome its deficiency in blue water shipping to constitute a credible threat to India.

China's interest in continued support to Pak including endorsement of General Musharaff's government, perhaps lies in the desire to maintain stability in Pak against the backdrop of rising Islamic fundamentalists. But one could also argue that China is more interested in keeping Islamabad under its influence against the influence of US rather than encouraging Pak to embark on reckless adventures.

The relations between two countries are on the rise. Last year during the visit of Chinese President Hu Jintao to Pak, 34 agreements and mamorandum of understanding to boost cooperation in private and public sectors were signed between the two heads of states. It was also announced by Pak to open its consulate in Chintaon, Capital of Pichwav province. Pak gives much importance to its relations with Western provinces including Pichwav. The economic and trade relations are said to be very close between the two and about ten projects including hydel projects and manufacturing of trains are underway at present. The Chinese President is reported to have also told Pak that China would continue to help Pak with its nuclear power industry but did not announce any new deal. He also promised to assit Pak with hydro-electric, coal and alternative source of energy. China has already helped develop Pak's Chashma-I nuclear power plant in Central Punjab and is willing to aid another one for similar type in Pak. The President of China also promised to view its relations with Pak from strategic and long term perspective and work together to elevate China-Pak strategic partnership to new hights. During his visit to one of the Chinese factories in Lahore, which manufactures air conditioners, refrigerators and other electronics items, the Chinese President declared that industrial cooperation with Pak will be further strengthened. He addressed the nation (Pak) live on TV from Islamabad. General Musharaff in return thanked the president of China for their help and cooperation in Karakoram highway, Gwadar Port, Chashma Power plant and supporting Pak's admission to the Asia Europe Meeting. General Musharaff further said that comprehensive cooperation and robust partnership between the two countries is in the fundamental interest of their people and conducive to peace, progress and stability in Asia.

One has to read in between the lines to see real Chinese aim in signing so many agreements with Pak and promising a long term strategic cooperation. Mr HU, President of China also visited India and signed 13 agreements here. This is most apparent improvement in the relations of India and China. On the nuclear front China has offered assistance to bolster India's nuclear energy for civilian purposes.

China and India have also made strides on defence matters. This includes port calls, joint exercises and defence exchanges. There are signs that Sino-Indo relations are also maturing fast as compared to Sino-Pak.

In the aftermath of September 11, Pak adopted a more aggressive policy towards China. This policy disguised as the fight against terrorism and helped US dislodge Taliban government. Pak even allowed some of its air bases for use by US troops for operations in Afganistan. China on the other hand perceived Pak to play an active role in cementing US hegemony adjacent to Chinese Western borders. China now feels ensnared by US military might stretching from the Asian Pecific to Afganistan.

The resurgence of political Islam across the muslim world has forced China to explore relations with the non-islamic countries. Since September 11, China has sought to expand security cooperation with Russia, Israel and India in a means of countering political Islam. All these factors have contributed to China's expansion of ties with India. But the eventual outcome of US-China-India-Pak relations hinges on three issues; one the ability of US to pull out of Iraq and Afganistan, two, Pak ability to organise control on its domestic and foreign policy from US and three–China's ability to emerge as a world power.

12

Pak Goes Nuclear

Pak nuclear policy began to evolve in real sense from 1955 onwards. In 1956 the Pak Atomic Energy Commission was established followed by the establishment of research councils. In 1957 a bilateral agreement was signed with USA for cooperation in the field of peaceful uses of atomic energy. It was later Mr Z A Bhutto who following the Bangladesh conflict of December 1971, convened a meeting of Pak nuclear Scientists in Multan in January 1972 and declared that never again should Pak allow India's superiority in conventional forces to give it an opportunity to repeat what it had done in December 1971. The scientists were instructed to devise plans to develop nuclear weapons, which would act as equalizer to match Indian conventional superiority. Soon after India's Pokhran's explosion in 1974 Pak quest for nuclear weapons began very seriously. Mr Z A Bhutto even said that Pak should have a bomb even if we have to eat grass. China agreed to assist Pak in developing nuclear weapons in 1976. Since then China has provided Pak with nuclear weapon designs and equipment for uranium enrichment and plutonium reprocessing. Pak has not looked back on its quest to acquire this might and its policy covering this aspect has undergone many upheavals.

The major phase of evolution of Pak's nuclear arsenal have generally been, as discussed in the sacceding paras.

Pre 1974

Broadly following aspects were covered by Pak in acquisition of nuclear capabilities.

(a) Build up scientific and technologial base within the financial resources.

(b) Development of nuclear energy for peaceful purposes.

(c) Support nuclear arms control measures and disarmanent proposals.

(d) Demand that India's nuclear facilities be put under international safeguards and inspections.

Bhutto Era

With Mr Z A Bhutto coming to power, Pak's nuclear policy underwent a perceptable shift with regard to the nuclear option, bilateral and international nuclear relations, nuclear arms control policies and safeguards. He articulated that only way to achieve power parity with India, was to develop the nuclear bomb. He opted for precurement of nuclear technologies, equipment and material through both overt and covert means. He established contacts with China and certain European countries to achieve his aim.

General Zia ul Haq

General Zia continued with the policies of Mr Bhutto, to start with, but subsequently in 1980 he modified his nuclear policy. In order to obtain international appreciation and recognition of its stance of peaceful intentions he opted to sign NPT and mutual renunciation of nuclear weapons alongwith India. He tried to islamise the bomb inorder to become the power centre in the Islamic world.

Ms Benazir Bhutto

Post Zia period, Benazir tried to project Pak's nuclear programme as one for the peaceful purposes and reiterated an offer of nuclear test ban and proposal to make South Asia a Nuclear Weapon Free Zone. During this period Pak continued calandestine operations to acquire nuclear equipment and material for its weapons related activities. It also made efforts to gain technology in the field of missile development and space research. The Hatf I and II were developed and publicity were made that Pak had modified F-16 aircraft to be able to carry nuclear weapons. It continued to produce weapons grade fissile material.

Mr Nawaj Shariff

He continued to follow the policies of his predecesors ie Zia and Benazir. Initiatives were taken to acquire nuclear plants from China and France. Pak admitted to procesing nuclear weapons, simultenously professing non proliferation and proposing CBMs towards India to withstand international pressure. However India's tests in May 1998 forced Pak to react and come out the closet by carrying out its own tests within two weeks of India, thus ending its policy of nuclear ambiguity.

Pak made a deal for a processing plant with France in 1976 but it was halted at a stage when blue prints had already been transfered to the former, due to US pressure not to go ahead with this project. This led France to offer the plant with a modified design which was however unacceptable to Pak. To conceal the real intentions, it was announced by Pak that it was in order to find an alternate source of energy in her nuclear power programme. Bhutto ordered the plutonium reprocessing plant from France, well aware of the fact that the west would assume that he would also use the plant to try to build an atom bomb. Infact he was determined to acquire a much more powerful hydrogen bomb which would depend on enriched uranium. Pak commenced her search for the know-how and the equipment to build the centrifuge. A coordinated operation was launched to get the equipment for a gas centrifuge uranium enrichment plant by precuring components from various European countries.

Pak Present Capabilities

After Pokhran II, in May 98, Pak followed suit by carrying out nuclear explosion at Changai Hills area in Baluchistan on 28 and 30 May 1998. This nuclear ambiguity prevaling before May 28 was no longer valid. Pak is likely to hold 16-20 nuclear bombs of 20 kt yield, deliverable by F-16 aircrafts, and missils. It is working towards enhancing its capabilities. Step being taken in this regard are:-

(a) Stepping up yield upto megaton.

(b) Acquire tactical nuclear weapons.

(c) Develop Second Strike Capabilities.

Pak bomb is India centric. It has adequate delivery means available to achieve its aim. With its present resources, it is able to cover entire sub continent. Its missile development programme with assitance from China is in advance stage. The delivery means that are available to Pak as on date are:-

(a) F-16 and mirage V aircrafts upto 500 kms.

(b) HATF missiles upto 800 kms.

(c) Missiles M-11, acquired from China

(d) Development of Gauri and Ghazanvi misslies with ranges upto 1600 kms.

Though Pak has not enunciated a formal nuclear doctrine, the head of the strategic planning division of its nuclear command Authority, told that Pak would make use of these weapons in the event of India capturing large part of Pak's territory. He also said that this contingency may also arise if India tries to economically strangulate Pak or pushes it to political distablization. On the other hand India has declared that it will not be the first to use nuclear weapons and will use nuclear weapons only if its territory or armed forces face an attack in which nuclear, chemical or biological weapons are used. Since India has no desire to conquer large parts of Pak's territories or destroy its armed forces, there is no possibility of India provoking a nuclear conflict. Pak is also aware that its Chinese supplied missile outmatch the missiles India presently has, but his entire Punjab province, the heartland of Pak fall well within the range of Indian Prithvi missiles. Though the Chances of use of nuclear weapons by either side are non existent but Pak's threats that its nuclear threshold is very low, and that it can also constantly bleed India, by low intensity conflict, without fear of retaliation by India, exist.

The pattern of Indo-Pak hostile relationship led Pak to perceive the Indian nuclear explosion as its intention to prematurely bring Pak under Indian domination. Pak views its nuclear assets as the country's only deterent against political and military bullying by India. The nuclear blackmailing would become more prominent.

Pak followed a calandestive approach to acquire the centrifuge. A cover organisation of the ordanance service of the government of Pak known as the special working organisation was created to conceal what Pak was doing. The vital equipment for the centrifuge plant was being calandistinely procured through a net work operating independent of Pak's diplomatic missions. The real work on the hydrogen bomb went on at Nellie in the Northern suburbs of Islamabd, where Pak Institute of Science and Technology worked on an experimental reactor, sealed from the public view.

Dr. A.Q. Khan the nuclear Scientist of Pak, by an unexplained breach of security was employed at Almelo in Holland in 1974-75 with access to extremely sensitive material. It was only three years after he returned to Pak that it was discovered that he had taken with him the secret for an advance pilot centrifuge which he subsequently duplicated at military compound at Kahuta. The pilot centrifuge is belived to be capable of producing, with in one year enough weapon grade U-235 for a single thermo-Nuclear explosion. Pak thereafter embarked on its major expansion of its nuclear weapons, it has set up a large extraction plant at Chasma and Khusab, a testing site at Changan hills. It is estimated that Pak has a stockpile of weapons grade uranium to build upto 50 nuclear devices. These devices are based on Chinese design.

Late Mr Bhutto had pronounced that he was endeavouring to make nuclear weapons in Pak for

Islamic civilization because the Christians, Jewish and Hindu civilization had already acquired the capabilities and communist power also possessed it. Most of the muslim states have signed and ratified the Non Proliferation Treaty (NPT). The significant no signatory to NPT are Pak and Saudi Arabia. Egypt has signed the NPT but has not ratified it. Besides, most of the muslim countries lack nuclear technology and industrial infrastructure and trained scientific manpower to undertake nuclear programme. Libya has been financing Pak's nuclear programme and also arranged supply of uranium from Islamic Republic Niger. It is believed that Niger is supplying 150 tons of Uranium concentration to Libya. Pak tried to gain position of leadership in Islamic block by being its sole nuclear power. China has also extended fule support to Pak's proposal fcr a five nation meet to resolve the nuclear proliferation issue in South Asia to make a nuclear free zone. China desires a multipolar management of non-proliferation regime.

Following revelations in the news media concering transfer of Pak nuclear technology to Iran, Libya and North Korea, Dr. A Q Khan in February 2004 admitted that he had overseen such transfer from the late 1980s until 2002. The Pak government said that Khan who had led its nuclear weapons program for quarter century had sold the technology for personal gains, but missiles parts were transfered at the same time from North Korea to Pak, leading arms experts from the world to believe that the government was at the very least aware of the transfers. But Khan was pardoned by General Musharaff since he is considerd Father of the Islamic bomb by Pak Janta.

In a democratic country like India control over nuclear weapon is well formulated and strictly adhered from the beginning, whereas in Pak the National Command Authority (NCA) to control Pak nuclear weapons was announced on 03 February 2000. This comprises of:-

(a) Strategic Planning Division to act as Secretariat.

(b) Employment control committee will be final deciding authority on employment of nuclear weapons.

(c) Development control committee will control development of strategic assets.

Chinese Assistance

China's missiles exports and assistance to Pak have been a serious proliferation over the years which includes transfer of complete M-11 missiles, missile related technology and manufacturing assistance to Pak. There is also a fear that Chinese technology and missiles may also be retransfered to third parties, further undercutting international non-proliferation efforts. The US has made serious efforts to dissuade China from transferring missils, components and missile related technology to Pak. US has approached China in a series of negotiation seeking to obtain Chinese pledges to abide by the Missile Technology Control Regime guidelines and eventually to become a member of the regime. Over the years China has provided Pak with a wide range of major conventional systems also to counter the Soviet and Indian security threats to self from Soviet and to Pak from India. This serves the two countries national security interest in the post cold war era. Pak relies on China as a trusted ally in dealing with India from a position of military weakness; China values its close ties with Pak both to extend influence to South Asia and to balance against India.

China despite its commitment continues to provide Pak with guidance system and technical expertise in its efforts to develop long range ballistic missiles. It has been speculated that the Shaheen-1, IRBM which Pak tested in April 1999, is actually modeled on Chinese M-9 missiles, China still continues to provide assistance to nuclear plant in Pak which was established with its aid. China whose experience in the construction of nuclear power station for commercial purpose was limited, it sought help and components from other countries. However under US pressure, Japan, Germany, France and other Western Countries refused to sell any component to China for use in the plant to be supplied to Pak. Hence the entire plant, except some minor component made in Pak were manufactured in China. China's help to Pak to upgrade its nuclear weapon capability continues despite pressure from US, which is matter of concern to all.

China is negotiating with Pak on an agreement to build the second stage of the Chashma nuclear power plant in Punjab province. The plant is for electricity generation and will be subject to the suspervision of the IAEA. The Chinese clarified that their country's cooperation with other countries in the area of nuclear technology was based on three principles, one – it must be for peaceful purposes, two – it must be under IAEA supervision and three – that without Chines approval, related technology can not be transferred to a third party.

Nuclear weapons in Asia are an irreversible reality for the foreseeable future except in the unlikely event of world moving towards universal and total disarmament. Given the islamic demensions of Pak's policies and rise of the Shia dominated Iran, proliferation from Pak to its western Islamic neighboures and to radical organisations like the Al-Qaeda can not be ruled out. In that event or in the event of Western fears that a future Islamist government in Pak may provide nuclear weapons potential to non-state actors, Pak could well face threats from those with whom it is allied today in the war on terror. The outcome of such a situation can well be understood by the sponsors.

For the whole period of the cold war, the world existed under the shadow of nuclear weapons and continues to do so in the post cold war era. The situation which threatened the very existance of world civilization also helped avert direct confrontation between two super powers. But even nuclear weapons continue to be regarded as a guaranter of peace, it is doubtful whether they will ever make anybody feel safe. Against this backdrop of global environment, which at best at the face of it was forcible advocating for preventing nuclear proliferation both vertically and horizontally. The nuclear tests in India and Pak have clearly demonstrated the pitfalls of such attempts.

Both India and Pak have strong motives to go nuclear. India's overwhelming superiority in conventional forces, its existing nuclear lead and Pak lack of strategic depth make the nuclear option very attractive for Pak. As regards India, her perception of herself on potentially great power and her committment to non alignment coupled with China's nuclear capability, made it almost mandatory for her to go nuclear.

Pak Nuclear Infrastructure

Pak nuclear program is based primarily on highly enriched uranium, which is produced at the A Q Khan research laboratory at Kahuta, a gas centrifuge uranium enrichment fecility. The Kahuta facility has been in operation since early 1980. By the early 1990s, Kahuta had an estimated 3000 centrifuges in operation and Pak continued its pursuit of expanded uranium enrichment capability.

In 1990, Pak began to pursue plutonium production capabilities. With the Chinese assistance, Pak built the 40 Mwt Khusab research at Johrabad and in April 1998, Pak announced that the reactor was operational. It is estimated that this unsafeguarded heavy water reactor generates an approximately 8-10 kilotons of weapon grade plutonium per year, which is enough for one to two nuclear weapons. The reactor could also produce tritium if it were loaded with lithium-6. According to reports, Khusab's plutonium production capacity could allow Pak to develop lighter nuclear warheads that would be easier to deliver with ballistic missiles. Plutonium separation reportedly takes place at a new laboratory reprocessing plant next to Pak Institute of Nuclear Science and Technology in Rawalpindi and at the larger Chasma nuclear power plant, neither of which is subject to IAEA inspection.

Pak Nuclear Doctrine

As per the reports, Pak's motive for pursuing a nuclear weapons program is to counter the threat posed by its main rival, India, which has superior conventional forces and nuclear weapons. Pak has not signed NPT and CTBT. Pak insists that India should sign these treaties first, then only it will consider. Pak also does not abide by a 'no-first use' doctrine, as was exhibited in General Musharaff's statement in May 2002 which said that Pak did not want a conflict with India, but that if it come to war between the two nuclear armed rivals, he would respond with full might. This statement was interpreted to mean that, if pressed by an overwhelming conventional attack from India, which has superior conventional forces, Pak might use its nuclear weapons.

Therefore, everyone world over is apprehensive that nuclear weapons in the hands of Pak, poses a danger to peace, not only in South Asia but all over. It may seen far fetched to the rational mind that some islamist faction within the Pak army itself, could seize and smuggle nuclear weapons or material for used in Jehad against India and western world.

13

Terrorism: Pak's Weapon of Strength

Introduction

Terrorism and the war on terror have paradoxical implications for Asian regional Stability. The results on war on terror in the region remains uncertain. While terrorism remains and will remain for sometime a challenge for regional countries, the nature and extent of this challenge will differ from country to country, thereby posing an obstacle to regional consensus and cooperation, including role of regional groups. It is difficult precisely how many terrorists are operating in and around Indian sub continent. The assessment of various agencies on the actual strength differs. There also exists considerable divergence among various countries over the defination of terrorism. In some part of Asia, perception of terrorist threat and national responses to it, are shaped by domestic concerns as well as political alliance compulsions. India views terrorism as a long standing problem that has only since 11th September 2001 begun to receive the recognition it deserved from the international community. India sees itself as the original setting or even a testing ground for terrorist tactics, citing examples of the 1993 bombing of the Mumbai Stock Exchange and December 1999 hijacking of an Indian Airlines flight by Pak nationals, forced to land in Afganistan, as precursors to the terrorist attacks on World Trade Centre in US. China also sees terrorism in terms of its own pre existing domestic security challenges.

Given the differing understanding of terrorism as a security threat, it should be hardly surprising that differences exist over counter terrorism strategy and resources channeled towards them even among countries where terrorism is perceived as a direct security threat. Asia's response to terrorism has been primarily at national and bilateral levels. An ASEAN declaration on 05 November 2001 called upon members to ratify all anti terrorist conventions including international conventions for the suppression of the financing of terrorism. ASEAN has also brought terrorism to the centre stage of its security agenda. Developing a common front against terrorism has been one of the objectives of the idea of ASEAN security community. But it is seen that at dealing with terrorism, regional groups have been better at issuing declarations and indentifying principles than developing concrete operational counter terrorism mechanism, which needs to be seriously done in the over all security interest of the region.

Pak and Terrorism

Pak knows that it can never match Indian conventional force. Therefore in order to compensate this inadequacy in their war machine she has resorted to sponsoring terrorism in the name of Jehad'. This of course has cost India dearly in terms of men and material. The act of terrorism are not only confined to the state of Jammu and Kashmir but also actualy spread all over India as a part of well thought out strategy of Pak leaders and is intimately controlled and executed by Pak ISI. On the other hand Pak has been gifted a few nuclear warheads by Chinese to deter India from resorting to any ill designs against Pak of which she very wrongly remains engrossed. Though India outmatches Pak on all counts, but what troubles India or the world is the apprehension of the nukes falling in the hands of terrorists of other fundamentalist in Pak who operate at a tangent with the central power of Pak. Pak's relations with China have been very friendly based on mutual strategic interest and common adversary. Pak also places great reliance on her relations with the other muslim countries. Some of them reciprocate positively to Pak's gestures and goodwill.

Indo-Pak relations have a long history of most suspicious, hatered, quinosity and religious divide. Tangible factors like Kashmir as well as intangible factors like emotions apprehensions and prejudices between these two nations deny them the ability to live in peace and harmony. Kashmir has been under the shadow of Pak sponsored militancy since 1989. These militants are divided in various groups based on different political agendas. Some press and help in making kashmir independent state whereas some want it to be the part of Pak. There is a large scale infiltration of foreign mercenaries, sponsered by Pak, from across the border. Pak's ISI spends about Rupees 60-80 crores every year for running a proxy war in Jammu & Kashmir (J&K), according to available reports. Besides misguided youths from J&K by ISI, a large number of heavily armed foreigner mercenaries are also operating, disguised as militants a civilian, collecting military intelligence about Indian defence forces.

There are following major known militant groups operating in J&K.

(a) Kashmir Hizbul Mujahideen with over 1000 men.

(b) Harkat-ul-Ansal with 350 men (Approximately)

(c) Laskar-e-Toiba with 300 men (Approx)

(d) Al Barg with 200 men (Approx)

(e) Al Jehad with 150 men (Approx)

There are a large number of training camps in Pak and POK. Some Islamic countries and organisations are funding the militancy in J&K, according to confirmed reports.

Though General Musharaff under the pressure from US after terrorist attack on World Trade Centre, has claimed banning Sunni militant Laskar-e-Jahangir and Shiite counterpart Sipah-e-Mohammad in August 2001. In January 2002 he banned some more groups, Jaise-e-Mohammad, Tahrik-e-Jafaria Pak, Sipahi-e-Sahaba Pak and Tehrik-e-Nufaz-e-Shariat-e-Mohammad. The last one was banned for leading the thousands of poor people into Afganistan and being responsible for their killings. These banned groups are generally all reorganised under new names. The Jamait-ud-Dawa was rechristened version of Laskar-e-Taiba. The banned Tehrik-e-Jafaria Pak has renamed itself as Tehrik-e-Islamia. Masood Azhar's Jaise-e-Mohammad has changed to Khudan-ul-Islam and Al Furqan. The Sepahi-e-Shahaba Pak led by Slim Azam Tariq is renamed as Milat-e-Islamia Pak. The Mackaz-ad-Dawa-wellaesahd now works under the name of Jammat-ad-Dawe.

In the murkey world of geopolitics Pak is both an ally in the war on terror and a fountainhead of Islamist militancy. General Musharaff under pressure from US arrested a few militants but released them later. Even after the US began counter terrorism operations inside Pak, the country remains a principle centre for terrorist training globally. Over the past year or so US, Labanon, Afganistan and UK have arrested suspected militants who either had training in Pak or were preparing to do so. UK unfolded a plot which would have attacked US bound airliner. UK categorised the suspects they arrested as 'homegrown' terrorists radicalized while living inside UK. But there was evidence that 24 suspects arrested, had tied to Pak and some had travelled there recently. A US official said some of the conceptualizing for the plot had occured in Pak. They were reported to be of Pak origin.

General Musharaff has been an intimate part of 'Jehad' which has become part of Pak army's part of philosophy over a period of time. Islamist groups appear to share a synergistic relationship with military rule. Army has helped build the Harkat-ul-Mujahideen which comprises the sinews of Osama Bin Laden's Islamic Jehad organisation. Sponsering terrorism in J&K is part of well thought out policy of Pak to gain an easy go at home. Though General Musharaff is fully aware that militant groups are not with him either for helping US led forces against Taliban in Afganistan but he is trying to keep a balance to keep even the fundamentalist happy.

The world on the other hand knows that Pak is maintaining double standard on terrorism. Though General Musharaff has shown his crackdown under US pressure and also that he himself has been attacked by them, however terrorist leaders have never been prosecuted, instead they have been placed in government safe houses and as a result these groups are up and operating under different names. Some of the terrorists who were arrested under world pressure were released later. Though General Musharaff again stage managed capture of Mullah Obaidullah Akhwnd, former defence minister of Taliban on 28 February 2007, from Quetta alongwith four others. Mr Obaidullah had a one million dollar bounty on his head. This was seen as a move by the military regime of Pak to release pressure of US who had been openly accusing Pak leadership for inaction and also of harbouring Taliban leaders in Pak. It is now to be seen as to what happens to this Taliban leader.

Continued Pak Help to Taliban

Pak is also not stopping anti Afgan activities being carried out from its territory. Mr Karzai has openly criticized and accused Pak of backing Taliban, which was ousted by US led forces. But General Musharaff, denies these allegations; though he did agree that some border guards had turned a blind eye towards Taliban fighters launching attack in Afganistan from Pak territory. Infact there were reports from Bagram (Afganistan) that an Afgan insurgent leader operating from inside Pakistan sent some 200 ill equipped fighters, some wearing plastig bags on their feet, into Afganistan where most of them were killed in a major battle against NATO forces. US forces killed one of the two groups, of about 130 fighters in the eastern province of Paktika, claimed to be the largest winter battles in Afganistan since the fall of the Taliban in 2001. Western and Afgan leaders accuse Pak of not doing enough to stop Taliban fighters using Pak soil for recruiting unemployed men, training them and sending them accross into Afganistan to fight. Though Pak says it does all it can to stop these people.

There were reports of about 700 foreign fighters, including Chechens, Pak and Uzbeks crossed over from Pak in Jan 2007 to reinforce Taliban guerrillas around key hydro-electric dam of Kajaki, where operations were on to clear rebels from the area, by the NATO forces. The dam is located in southern Helmand province of Afganistan. During this action, Taliban extremists resorted to the use of human shields, specifically using local Afgan children to cover their movement out of this area.

Islamic militants were consolidating their hold in northern Pak, vastly expanding their training of suicide bombers and other recruits and fortifying alliances with Al-Queda and foreign fighters; it has proved as a mini Taliban state. The militant are taking advantage of peace deal of September 2006 in North Waziristan under which they agreed to end cross border help for the Taliban insurgency, and they are openly flouting the peace deal. The area is becoming a magnet for an influx of foreign fighters, who do not only challange government authority in the area, but are even wresting control from local tribes and spreading their influence to neighbouring areas according to US intelligence.

In a strikingly strong language, Afgan President Hamid Karzai said that failure to bring peace to Afganistan would destroy the whole region and he laid blame on neighbouring Pak. In another statement he said that Pak leadership is trying to turn his countrymen into slaves by incitig wave of violence. He even told that Mulah Omar the supreme Taliban leader who headed the representative Islamist regime, ousted by US led forces five year ago, is hiding in the Pak city of Quetta.

US Chief Intelligence, John Negroponte also told that Al Qaeda leaders are holed up in secure hideouts in Pak from where they were revitalising their bruised but resitient network. They are cultivating stronger operational connections and relationship that outflows from their leaders secure hideouts. There are also reports that Al Qaeda leader Osama Bin Laden and his second in command Ayman-al-Zawahiri are hiding somewhere along the rugged mountainous border between Pak and Afganistan.

Infact the media is totally forbidden in the area of operation and hence no first hand information is coming out. Last year Carlotta Gall, a New York Times correspondents was reportedly assaulted by Pak ISI and was warned not to interview the Taliban.

General Musharaff is trying hard to make world believe that he is earnestly trying to control the trans-border movement into Afganistan and that no assistance is being provided by his government to the insurgents. Pak has reported to have opened its first biometric systems to screen travellers at a border point with Afganistan as a measure to curtail cross border movement of militants. The system was installed at the main border crossing between Southern Afganistan and Pak's South western Baluchistan province, near the Pak town of Chaman. This is one of the measures to fight terrorism, claimed the Pak authorities. Pak army even carried out airstrike on a madrasa in the tribal area based on US intelligence and killed 80 people in November 2006 who were called insurgents, hiding there. There was a mass protest by tribesmen of the area supported by MMA (Pak Political Party) against this operations. Pak has deployed about 80,000 troops along Pak-Afgan border to track down militants as told by them.

Ethnic Pashtun tribesmen in Pak and Afganistan living close to the border of two countries, are allowed to travel across the frontier without passports but with special identity permits under an arrangement between the two countries to help the members of the divided tribes visit each other. The Afgan-Pak border runs through rugged mountains, deserts and is not clearly demarcated at places where it splits the tribes people. Last year, Pak announced that it will build fence and plant land mines at sections of the border to stop illegal cross-border movement. It was opposed by Afgan people saying that it will not stop terrorism but will only divide the tribes.

Mr Karzai, who came to power after Taliban regime fell in late 2001, but has been seriously involved in controlling the militant violance in Afganistan, accused that Taliban has sanctuaries in Pak and large number of them are hiding in Karachi and Miran Shah in north Wazirstan, a lawless border region where Pak government recently reached a peace deal with pro-Taliban militants after mediation by tribal elders.

Even Iran is apprehensive of the fallouts towards their country. They are building a concrete wall along its frontier to stop illegal border crossings. The wall will start from Taftan to Mand along the entire Iran-Pak border; Taftan is about 700 kms west of Quetta, the capital of Balochistan. As revealed by Pak official the wall whose construction has already begun, would be 10 feet high and three feet wide.

Terrorism in India

Mumbai blast brought in focus once again that Pak proxy war against India and use of Islamist regions terrorism, based in Pak, continues unabated. These terrorist groups are trained, patronized and financed by Pak ISI. The response of US on terrorists act in India was disappointing, which was politially motivated not to condemn Pak, but morally was highly incorrect. It was only after bombing of World Trade Centre in US, that some kind of heat was felt globally by the acts of terrorism. But it became amply clear to India that this menace of Pak sponsered terrorism has to be dealt firmly by itself.

Some of the major terrorist attacks which took place in India are discussed in the succeding paragraphs.

(a) 01 October 2001. Militants attacked Jammu & Kashmir State assembly complex, killing 38 people including civilians.

(b) 13 December 2001. Attack on Indian Parliament in New Delhi which left nine security personnel killed. The terrorists who were also killed were identified as Pak nationals. This attack was aimed at crippling the Indian government at least for sometime, since there were approximately 200 members of Parliament inside.

(c) 24 September 2002. Militants attacked Akshardham temple in Gujrat, 31 people including a few security personnel were killed.

(d) 29 October 2005. Number of serial bomb blasts took place in Delhi in areas of Paharganj, Sarojini Nagar and Govindpuri. Approximately 70 people including children died in these ghastly blasts.

(e) 11 July 2006. At least 200 people were killed in train blast in Mumbai and over 700 were injured. This shook India's financial capital badly.

(f) 8 February 2007. Bomb blasts took place in Samjhauta Express near Panipat (Haryana) When it was on its way to Atari border from Delhi. Indians as well Pak nationals died in the attack. This was probably aimed at derailing peace process talks which were schdules to take place in New Delhi the next day between the two countries. However the way Pak took away their injured from the hospital in Delhi by an PAF plane, to avoid interrogation by Indian authorities point fingure of suspicion on Pak ISI.

There are also reports that Terror groups operating with the support of Pak have resorted to carefully chartered manipulation of Indian stock market through fake companies to raise funds to finance terrorism against India. This fact was revealed by Mr M.K. Narayanan, the national adviser at Munich, while speaking at a conference on International security. Mr Narayanan spoke of a conspiracy by official agencies in Pak (ISI), for the plot to carryout economic subversion and raising funds within India to strike against the country. He also gave out the complex mix of funding routes-through stock exchanges, banking channels, ordinary ATM withdrawls and Hawala trails as well as operation of legitimate businesses like hotels and transport.

Terrorism in Kashmir has existed in various forms which has taken a heavy toll on the Indian security forces and civilian population of J&K. Other than the drain on Indian economy and manpower the insurgency has undermined the democratic values. This has had an adverse impact on the growth rates in the State of J&K and has led to an increased sense of alienation. This has also adversely affected the social cohesion of society in J&K.

Islamic terrorism in India is also a by product of US, who inspired young mercernaries to fight Soviets in Afganistan. This was given the name of Jehad against communism. The majority of muslim over hundred went to Afganistan to fight against Soviet troops from J&K, only a very small number was from other part of India. They now have become hardcore members of banned, Student's Islamic Movement of India (SIMI). They are being prompted by ISI against India, who were their monitors in Afganistan. Though the number of indigenous militants supported and persuaded by Pak ISI, is small but is steadily increasing. The policy of secularism inhibits India's strong move against such misguided citizens of a particular community, lest should such over reaction on part of the government drive law abiding muslims in the hand of extremists. The vast majority of Indian muslims are nationalists, patriotic and do not associate themselves with the antinational elements in their community. India is a witness to long standing and better conflict between India and Pak. What Pak views as the political destinies of people of J&K, India views it as her territorial integrity. Though

Pak leadership of late has been giving assurance of not allowing terrorists group use it soil but it is obivious that unless Pak takes concrete steps to implement the solemn assurance it has given to prevent cross border terrorism against India, all efforts towards peace process will be undermined.

The biggest challange in the war against Pak sponsered terrorism is India's inhibition to deal firmly with it. India needs to get over her defensive mindset and assert her true might in a manner free of all historical hang ups. India needs to appreciate that crying about evil of terrorism is futile and India needs to find out its own way to deal with the situation. Our leadership has to be involved totally and has to exhibit certain firmness while formulating policies to counter terrorism, rising above party politics in the interest of the country. There should not be a shift in our stand as presently seen in various briefings by the government. Indian Prime Minister Mr Manmohan Singh while talking about war on terror in Mumbai, the otherday said, "we are certain these terror modules are instigated, inspired and supported by elements across the border without which they can not act with such a devastating effect, the time has come for us to crack down and destroy all these antinational elements. We will leave no stone unturned in ensuring that terrorists elements in India are nuetralized and smashed." But little later when the PM returned from G-8 summit in July 2006, there appeared: slight change in his approach toward 'softer side. This needs to be avoided otherwise India will never get rid of the menace of terrorism. India's soft diplomacy is seen as a weakness by these elements.

Also all other countries in our region must recognise that terrorism anywhere is a threat to peace and prosperity every where. It therefore must be confronted with united efforts.

Pak's Jehadi Policy Backfires

Rearing a terrorist is akin to mounting a wild tiger who would take on the rider soon he dismounts. The same is begining to unfold in case of Pak's Jehad policy. Most of the terrorist groups are deadly against General Musharaff's policy of helping the US led forces against Taliban in Afganistan; and he has hardly a control over these groups and also on its intelligence outfit ie. ISI who has grown 'too' big for the Pak leadership to manage. General Musharaff has faced three attacks including suicide bombing which nearly took him on. His enemies today are the same extremists that Pak army nurtured first against the Soviets and now against India. There were also reports that some of the personnel of General Musharaff's own inner security ring abetted these attacks on him. Several young officers with the Pak Air Force with access to President Musharaff's inner most security circle were among 50 people arrested for trying to assassinate him. The rocket strike was aimed at the President's high security personal residence office in Rawalpindi in September 2006. Those arrested are believed to have acted out of growing anger at General Musharaff's alliance with US in its war on terror. While General Musharaff relies on the armed forces to keep him in power but it is believed that junior and middle rung officers are losing faith in his leadership because of his open help to NATO forces and the US.

Pak's policy of using Jehadi terrorists to achieve tripple strategic objectines- to acquire strategic depth by controlling Afganistan, to counter successionist trends in NWFP and Sindh and most importantly to harass India is fraught with serious risk for Pak itself. The suicide bomb attacks in Pak had demonstrated both the growing reach of Jehadi elements as well as the vulnerability of Pak heartland, the fortified Islamabad. The rash of recent terrorist incidents in Pak, in the latest of which a suicide bomber blew up a courtroom in Quetta Killing 16 people, indicates that Pak is now reaping what it has sown. There were also reports of Pak authorities demolishing two mosques in Islamabad which was located on main road, to prevent them from being used to launch terrorists attacks on passing dignitaries. Over 300 religious leaders protested the demolitions, with some denouncing the action as an attempt by General Musharaff to impress the US with its anti terrorism efforts.

It is therefore prudent for the leadership in Pak to realize the folies they have committed/committing, lest should these engulf the entire Pak into its clutches. Terrorism does not respect international borders and the islamist terrorism that is the main tool of mobilization in Pak's covert war against India is a universal ideology that recognizes US as one of the foremost enemies. If Islamist terrorism succeeds anywhere in the world, it will repeat itself anywhere.

The recent turn around in Pak economy can largely be attributed to US and flowing into Pak since 9/11. They should not only be the reason that Pak should apply itself to countering the militant Islamist threat. The fact of the matter is that it is in Pak's own interest to purge the militants from its soil. If terror outfit should continue to operate from its tribal regions, the US may well change its policy and start operations inside Pak territory to liquidate the terrorists.

US drone attacks on militant Madarasas in Bajpur last year was only a pointer to things that may follow. It would therefore be much better if Pak moved to subdue militants within its own terriroty. Calling tribal areas ungovernable is no excuse; it is very much part of Pak territory. Pak should chase Taliban out of its area and also purge its own intelligence services, particularly ISI.

14

Internal Strife in Pak

Introduction

Pakistan comprises of four province, two territories and administers part of Kashmir. There is a vast difference in the culture and economic status among these four provinces which are the basic reasons of continued turmoil in Pak. Some the peculiarities of these provinces are discussed in the succeding paragraphs. The turncated borders of Pak, consists of four major ethnic groups – Punjabis, Sindhis, Pashtuns and Baluchs and several other ethnic groups, Mojahir in Southern cities of Karachi and Hyderabad, Kashmiris in North and Saraiki speaking groups in the middle. Pak borders four countries, Afganistan, Iran, China and India. The border with each of these countries is problematic. The border with Afganistan is based on Duran Line, arbitrarily demarcated by the Britishers in 19th century. Pashtuns, who were historically united live on both sides of the mountainous border. The border with Iran is mostly populated by Baluch tribes who live in a large sparsely populated desert on both sides of the border. The Baluchis in Pak demanded autonomy in 1970s and thousands were massacred by army.

The Baloch and Pashtun embraced islam at a very early period and strove for equality with the competing tribal groups, like Arabs, Kurds and Turks. They also retained much of their pre-islamic tribal culture and language, which their descendents proudly carried down intact to this day. The Punjabis, Sindhis and Mohajirs were converted by the invading armies of Arabs and Turks and were forced to adopt some of their cultural traits. The Baloch and Pashtuns share many affinities. Both were tribal groups that had not got modernised even under British raj. The conservative societies were marked with gun and agriculture. They never tried together to get a better deal from Punjabi dominated Pak government. The Punjabis infact made them fight with each other. The focal point is of Punjabis domination in the army. Seventy percent of the army in Pak is drawn from three Punjab districts (Rawalpindi, Jhelum, Campbellpur) and two adjacent districts in NWFP (Kohat and Mardan).

Punjab Province

This is the dominating province of Pak. Punjabis are in the upper echelon of the society and hold majority of senior posts in civil and military. This situation is resented by many Pakhtuns, Baloch and particularly by Sindhis, whose numbers of wealth are comparitively small and who are proportionately unrepresented in public positions.

Most Punjabis link their ancestry to pre islamic Rajputs and Jats casts. They are a coherent ethnic community that has historically placed great emphasis on farming and fighting.

North West Frontier Province (NWFP)

NWFP is identified with Pakhtuns which is one of the largest tribal groups in the world. This is the smallest of the four provinces of Pak and is a home to the Pashtuns (Afgans) and various other groups. They are in Balochistan and also in Southern Afganistan. They are organised in segmentary clans. Most Pakhtuns are pious Sinni muslims. Since 1980s many Pakhtuns have entered the police, civil services, military and are dominating the country's transport business. A growing number of projects in NWFP have also provided diverse employment opportunities to Pakhtuns.

The neighbouring regions of NWFP include Afganistan to the West and North and Northern areas of Azad Kashmir (POK) to the NE and East. The federally administered tribal areas stand buffer between the NWFP and parts of Afganistan and Baluchistan. Punjab and Islamabad Capital territory are to the South and East. The main language is Pashto and the provincial capital is Peshawar. The NWFP traditionally was part of Afganistan, but was divided during the British rule of India. The NWFP remained heavily influenced by the events in Afganistan and civil war led to the rise of Taliban which had emerged in the border region between Afganistan and Pak as a formidable political force. Since the US led operations against Taliban, NWFP has become a frontline State.

The main cities are Dera Ismail Khan, Kohat, Bannu, Peshawar and Hazara. The region varies in topography from dry rocky area in the south to forests and green plains in the North.

Balochistan

The province of Balochistan is the largest of the all the provinces of Pak. To its west is Iranian Balochistan, to the North are Afganistan and federally administered Tribal areas of Pak, Punjab and Sindh are to the East and to the South is Arabian sea. The population density is very low due to the mountainous terrain and scarcity of water. The state capital is Quetta. The port of Gwadar where Pak government is undertaking a large project with Chinese help to build a large port is part of this province. The important cities are Khuzdar, Turbat, Chaman, Sibi, Gwadar, Zhob, Pasni, Kharan, Kalat and Mastung.

Baloch is comparatively a small clan. They are also spread in large areas however major Chunk live in

Pak. The others are in Iran and Afganistan. The area of Balochistan is hard and rugged to live and subsist on. The main source of livelihood is on keeping large herds of sheeps and goats. They are also Sunnis. They are characterised as 'Feudal Militarism'. They are generally hospitable people. The power structure concentrates in the hands of local tribal leaders. There have been spordic separatist movements in Balochistan since independence. They have long been accustomed to indirect rule, a policy that leaves local elite with substantial measure of autonomy.

Sindh

This is also one of the four provinces of Pak. The neighbouring regions are Balochistan to the West and North, Punjab in the North and Rajasthan (India) to the East. To the South are Arabian sea and Rann of Kutch. Sindh is the third largest province of Pak geographically. Historically Sindh has been a very rich region. It was here that first urban civilization developed in 3000 BC at Mohanjodaro. The state capital is Karachi. The other important cities are Hyderabad, Sukkur, Tando Adam, Nwab Shah, Larkana, Shikarpur, Khairpur and Badin. Languages spoken include Sindhi, Landa, Urdu and Rajasthani. This province was incorporated into Pak in 1947.

This has been a neglected area since British raj. The landlords dominated the society where most of the people were employed on contract basis by the

Zamindars. Middle class was almost non-existent. There was considerable upheaval in Sindh in the years following partition. Millions of Hindus and Sikhs migrated to India and a large number of muslims (known as Mujahirs) came from India to this area. They later formed into political party known as Mujahir Qaumi Maha (MQM). The cities of Larkana, Thatta and Hyderabad became centre of Sindhi resistance. In 1994 Sindh continued to be an ethnic battlefield within Pak. During 1980s there were repeated kidnapping and political provocations. The area is generally unsafe to travel by road due to fear of dacoits etc.

The controversial history of the South Western region of Pak dates back the time when the Durand Line was drawn by the British in 1893 after fighting two wars in Afganistan. The border was drawn to divide the Pashtun and Baloch tribes of the area into international borders of Iran, Afganistan and what later became West Pak. The Balochis found their nomadic ways disrupted by the division created by the international border and were not happy with the outcome and hence the seeds of strife were sown.

The Strife

Intrigues, usurpation of power by force, suppression of citizen's rights and aspirations in the name of Islam and belied hopes sum up the history of Pak. The country has not been able to establish a one nation identity, although ironically created in the name of two nations, theory, which said Hindus and Muslims were two different nations. On the contrary the gulf between its federating provinces has been increasing which is due to perpetual military rule-with Punjabi dominance. Strong feeling of alienation among minority provinces of Sindh, Baluchistan and NWFP was amply demostrated during civil disobedience movement launched for Restoration of Democracy in 1983. The demand was rearrangement of Pak as a confederation of autonomous and sovereign provinces in keeping with the 1940 Lahore resolution of muslim league.

During the civil disobedience, the Baluchs and Sindhis had developed a great feeling of fraternity as fellow sufferers at the hands of Punjabi army. The Baluchs suffered in 1963 during Ayub's regime and then from 1973 to 1977 during Bhutto's rule at the hands of army. Thousands of young Baluchs crossed over to Afganistan looking for a right opportunity to strike back.

In Sindh, the civil disobedience movement took shape of total uprising involving all sections of the Sindhi society. They too suffered heavily at the hands of Pak army. Sindhi youth complain of discrimination and exploitation. Even the Sindhi PPP leaders desire an autonomy, though not openly. Mrs Benazir Bhutto's casual remarks at number of times, talk of deprivation among minority provinces. But obiviously she will not finish her political career by openly advocating provincial autonomy. But her cousine Mumtaz Ali Bhutto openly came out with a scheme of confederation.

In NWFP too there was a similar demand for independence Pakhtunistan on the eve of civil disobedience movement launched by the Movement For Restoration of Democracy (MRD). In Punjab too there has been an undercurrent of Punjabi nationalism particularly by Ghulam Mustafa Khar who was removed from CM of Punjab by Mr Z A Bhutto.

Continuous suppression of democracy, human rights, civil liberties and non stoppage of military domination are forcing minority provinces to seek their own separate ways. The military tries to eliminate such political leaders either by long term imprisonment without substantial charges, banning their inter provincial movement or forcing them into exile abroad. Though the new generation which do not have all Pak national view and are more exposed to extrenal influences than their elders, can no longer be exploited in the name of Islam and ideology of Pak; no matter how much brain washing is done through education system/ madarasas. Since the army does not respect any constitution, this young generation may use unconstitutional means to get rid of military rule. In any case these tribal areas are essentially autonomous with little government presence and are governed largely by tribal traditions and councils.

The Parliamentary system outlined in 1956 constitution required disciplined political parties which did not exist. The muslim league only political party which endeavoured to promote democracy was gradually declining in popularity. In West Pak, Sindh and NWFP resented political and economic dominance of Punjab, over a period, sometime, in mid fifties, societal violance and ethnic unrest further complicated the growth and functioning of Parliamentry government. In West Pak, Chief Minister Khan Sahib was assassinated. In NWFP, Khan's brother Khan Abdul Gafar Khan of National Awamy Party turned his back on national politics and announced that he would work for the attainment of a separate homeland for the Pakhtuns. In Baluchistan the Khan of Kalat again declared his independence, where Pak army restored Pak control.

The demand of minority provinces for separation is more an expression of anger and frustration, though many may still not want to part company from Pak. But this lot of people could be driven to helplessness if minority provinces are not given their due.

Baluchistan has been a flashpoint throughout. They have long been accustomed to indirect rule, a policy that leaves local leaders with a substantial measures of autonomy. 1970s, saw a precipitious detrioration in relation with central government of Pak. The voilent confrontation between Baloch insurgents and Pak military was very serious. The demands of greater regional autonomy escalated into full scale movement aimed at restructuring the government on the confederal lines. Baluchistan landscape changed immensely as Afgan refugees camps were established throughout the northern parts of the province. In many places 'kacha' thatched houses got converted into concrete structures. These refugees also affected demographic balance as some of them permanently settled in Baluchistan itself. There is very little progress and development in the area because of limited population; social condition, in the rural areas have very marginally changed.

In view of the present involvement of Pak in the war on terror against Taliban in support of US led forces, it is anyone's guess what would be the end of the act; whether these tribal provinces will remain with Pak or will fight their way out for autonomy alongside Taliban. Weapons given by the US, to fight Al Qaeda and Taliban are being used by Pak military to fight tribesmen in the restive Balochistan province, as reported by a local Baluch leader. There was a tribal violance in protest against the killing of Balochi leader Nawab Akbar Khan Bugti by the Pak army, allegedly located his hideout using advanced US equipment. The Pak army initially claimed success in killing Mr Bugti, but following public anger, they attributed his death to the collapse of a cave in which he was hiding.

Balochistan has a long history of Strife. Despite being the largest province with significant natural resources, it has remained extremely poor since its incorporation into the newly created Pak against the wishes of its people. The army actions by military rulers have further fuelled a sense of deprivation and desire for a greater autonomy. Pak's Human Rights Commission has cited hundreds of cases of torture, abduction, disappearance and deaths of many political leaders and other important people of the province. The present crisis is attributed to General Musharaff's plans to develop oil and natural gas fields, build an oil pipe line across the region and construct a strategic deep sea port to expand trade with China. The Baloches are not against the economic development of the area but have accused Islamabad of paying meager royalties for the resources. Energy installation have become primary targets of Balochi rebels. Former Air Chief Martial Ashgar Khan Condemned Mr Bugti's killing and said that his death would have serious implications for the unity and integrity of Pak. Even government of Pak came under fire from the opposition coalition for this innocent killing.

The roots of ethnic conflict in Pak also lie around Karachi and other urban region of Sindh, where Mohajirs who failed to build a common religious bond with other population groups. Being the forefront of the struggle for Pak, they were naturally in a dominant position at the time of partition and were the ardent supporters of Pak nationalism, as opposed to the regional identities professed by Sindhis, Pathans and Punjabis. Mohajir's dominance in Pak's politics was gradually eroded by the Punjabi bureaucratic-military clique and federal power gradually shifted to Punjab. Thereafter there have been periodical clashes between

Mojahirs and other ethnic minorities ie. Pathan and Sindhis. The Mojahirs do not get a fair deal from the government agencies including state police. The MQM's agenda has been to get a better deal for the Mojahirs from Punjabi centre and from the Sindhi provincial government, which it perceives as oppressive.

In Pak one can easily conclude that religious and ethnic organisations representing their respective communities are increasingly using violent methods including terrorism. In the past number of years the Afgan war has also negative impact on internal strife in Pak. Its ramifications include the growth of various islamic groups that have involved in running the feuds between Sunni and Shia organisations and the mafia operating in Pak poses a threat to its security in the times to come.

In March 2004, Pak army began operations against foreign islamic militants in South Wazirstan, but the local military who regarded the attacks as a breach of their local autonomy, found in the fight against the Pak army. The fighting continued in 2005, when operations were also began in North Waziristan. Agreements with tribal leaders in both regions ended military operations in Waziristan in late 2006. Fighting also occured in Baluchistan, where local tribes demanded a greater share in the province's mineral wealth and an end of stationing military force in that area. The fighting in that area also continued till end of 2006.

The massacre of 53 members of the Hazara tribe (who are Shias) at Quetta the capital city of Balochistan, while they were praying, by some unidentified gunmen in July 2003. Soon thereafter 11 Hazaras who were police trainers were also killed in Quetta itself. This is seen as an attempt by Taliban and Al Qaeda operatives, who have take shelter in Pak's tribal area, to drive out Hazaras who are Shias, from this area lest they be used by US intelligence agencies to collect information about the presence of Osama Bin Laden and his associates in the tribal belt of NWFP and Balochistan. It is also seen as an effort to ignite cycle of violance between Shias and Sunnis, in order to destablize Pak.

The Northern areas of Pak occupied Kashmir have also witnessed violent protests against junta's decision to introduce the islamic carriculum in the educational institutions. The local Shia community is agitated over this government move to introduce the new carriculum because it was in conflict with their school of thought. The protesting mob tried to close down army run schools in Gilgit. The Shia leaders said that text books (Islamic Studies) promote Sunni thought and totally neglect Shias. They feel it has been deliberately done to promote sectarian hatered between the two sects. Pak assuemed control of Northern area soon after partition in 1947 and it administered them under the Frontier Crime Regulations. The Northern areas are part of POK, its writ was never allowed to run there. The people there have no recourse to courts either in POK or Pak. Although the Northern areas are part of J&K, Pak transfered 2500 Sq miles of its area to China under the Pak-China boundary agreement of 1962. It is in this context the people of Northern areas have started a movement to free themselves from the military rule of Pak. This being done by all political parties ie. Gilgit-Baltistan National Alliance and other groups.

Though Pak always doubts Indian intentions, but it has been accepted by everyone including US and India that united Pak is desirable, even necessary for the stability in the region. Several reasons are commonly advanced for this position; one that dissolution of Pak would encourage divisions within India, two – It would result in an uncertain future of nuclear weapons presently being controlled by the military regime of Pak and finally US feels Pak can always serve as a useful client or proxy in the war against terrorism. The ideas floated by Mr Sayed Jamaluddin in his book titled 'To Eliminate Terrorism Divide Pak' are untenable and wild in the present context.

Shias make upto over ten percent of population in Pak, Christians upto five percent and Sunnias are nearly eighty percent of the population. Both the Sunnis and Shias. sects over a period of time have developed their own political organisations. The Sunni organisations being the biggest have further fragmented into sub groups. Militant groups of both sects have in the past targeted each other's members but the last few years have seen an upserge of systematic killing of people unconnected with the sectarian strife, particularly in Karachi. The proportion of Shia's minority victims has been high. The minority sect is angered over the weak response of Pak government to the ghastly situation. Though General Musharaff has on several occasions condemned sectarian violence and has banned several sectarian groups. But the terrorism and secretarianism is far from being under control.

Conclusion

In overall analysis of the entire profile, Pak needs to develop a comprehensive strategy to regain control over terrorism which they have inadvertantly allowed to breed in internal politics of Pak also. This unless treated as a serious threat by Pak government to their national security problem, the country will get distablized in near future.

US should also realize that they are blindly trusting one man and have put all eggs in one basket with rapidly diminishing returns. It is true that some Al Qaeda terrorists have been arrested with the help of Pak, but is it enough in return of massive supports US has given to that country. It is also very clear that anti-US islamist are in charge of NWFP and Baluchistan governments and terrorists operate more or less openly in Pak. Taliban and Al Qaeda are carrying out raids from Pak as well recruiting openly in Deoband madrasas. Is it that what US expects from Pak?

President of Pak still seems to bank upon the old wisdom that the legitimacy and power of a Pak ruler is derived from three sources ie Army, America and Allah - Pak's Punjabi dominated army in search of the elusive purity and to prepetuate its hold on power structure encourages the majority Punjabi Sunni population in its misadventures. In persuit of power, the bogey threat from India was always played upon. In schools children are taught to hate Indian. Therefore the gensis of the Pak present fault lies in their mindset which has engineered trouble for the entire world and is waiting for self inflicted injuries to occur.

A good general can intelligently anticipate the real move and a motive behind a faint. It is paradoxically less easy to do so against unsophisticated tribemen, brimming over with more bravado than brain. General Musharaff therefore has to apply total wisdom while dealing with tribals of Baluchistan and NWFP. The military ruler has immense powers, but he is also constrained in practice by strong centre of support for islamic militancy in the Pak officers corps and hardliner islamic groups that have prolifirated across Pak.

Pak's porous border with Afganistan has facilitated the trans shipment of men and material with impunity. The territory contiguous with the border are formally designated 'Tribal Agencies, semi-autonomous regions, administered directly by a political agent appointed by the Federal government. The ethnic identity of the population in the agencies is for all practical purpose identical to that across the border in Afganistan. The less formal administration of these agencies has fecilitated a variety of cross border activities and smuggling.

Pak's cooperation in a military action in Afganistan is crucial for US because the absence of any other US bases on Afgan border and because access to land locked, mountainous country from any where else would be arduous or near impossible.

15

INDO-PAK RELATIONS

The relations between India and Pakistan have been strained even since the two got separated in 1947. There is a considerable difference of opinion over the reasons underlying Pak's hostile attitude and her apparently self induced paranoic fear of India. Some feel that the Kashmir issue is the root cause and that once this is settled an era of peace and cooperation may ensue. On the other hand some are of the view that the seeds of conflict spring from the very logic behind partition and that for a foreseeable future there can only be an armed truce between theocratic muslim Pak and secular but Hindu dominated India. In support of the later view, it is also argued that the unique distinction that history bestowed on Pak in constituting two widely separated wings, people of the East were ethnically completely different and much closer to Indian population living across the border, has since been liberated by India and a new state of Bangladesh has come into being. The has added to already existing hatred of partition which Pak very grudgingly harbour against India.

The roots of Pak insecurity can, infact be traced back to British colonial policy of divide and rule which in many ways both planted and later fawned rivalries between Indian National Congress and the Muslim League, leading finally to creation of two separate states. It was the same psyche that was later responsible for Islamabad seeing itself as the loser, both in division of assets and because Kashmir acceded to India. This was followed by claim of bad events which led to sense of insecurity in Pak. From the military point of view the division of British India was potentially dangerous for Pak. The Japanese advance during Second World War had demostrated the vulnerability of the eastern frontier. East Pak had indefensible borders with Burma and mostly surrounded by India. From the beginning it was a strategic liability for Pak, a new nation. The turbulent North West, which became part of Pak had been traditional invasion route into India. Russian expansion via Afganistan is a constant danger to Pak.

Pak's foreign policy is preoccupied with India and fear of Indian invasion. This policy has been helping her to manage aid from US time and again. Though US policy in providing aid to Pak may not conform to the latter's thinking, but whatever be the reasons, they have been benifitting. The islamic world also provides Pak with both tangible and intangible sources of support. Pak has relied heavily on Islamic solidarity as a protective shield against communist expansion, even via afganistan.

The legacy of suspicion and mistrust predates the independence of the two countries. At the same time both countries face serious national challanges of socio-economic development which require an environment of peace and stability at the very minimum, and preferable friendship at the optimum level. The hostility confrontation and conflict are essentially the products of peprceptions heavily influenced by mistrust and psychological barriers. This aspect needs to be looked into seriously by both the countries if they wish to remain in peace.

Pak's relations with China have been friendly based on mutual interest and common adversary. Pak preoccupied with India, certainly weigh Indian actions and policies carefully in selecting a course to follow. The attitude of the outside world to Pak, plays a significant role in helping her in selecting a course; put in final analysis Pak's position would always be reactive to Indian policy. She cannot afford a big venture against India, but will continue playing pin pricks by way of terrorism and continue gaining outside aid and sympathy by keeping Kashmir issue alive. Mostly it is seen that Pak's policies in regard to India are essentially emotional and are not based on any substantial reasons.

The Kashmir issue evokes such a strong emotional response in the people of Pak and India and two governments are so deeply committed to their respective stances that the prospect of an amicable settlement are indeed remote. The wars of 1965, 1971 and later of course in Kargil operation, clearly demonstrated India's determination as well her ability to prevent Pak from altering the status quo by military force and at the same time highlighted the face that India harboured no territorial ambitions against Pak. It has also probably brought to the outside world that any attempts to coerce India were unlikely to succeed and would instead be counter productive. It is infact the undue military aid to Pak to maintain a balance of power in the sub continent, which is one of the root causes of instability in the relation of two countries. The Chinese who are also helping Pak by providing nuclear arsenal only stand to gain in overall power balance in Asia which is against the interest of the West.

The proxy war by Pak in J&K is certainly a heavy drain on Indian economy. This is likely to continue since it serves Pak's national interests at no cost. She tries to keep Kashmir issue alive and internationalize time and again. This also provides her an excuse to sponser terrorism in the name of Jehad. However of late the militant movement in Kashmir is yielding deminishing returns to Pak. Popular participation and enthusiasm have declined. Azadi is no more round the corner as the people of Kashmir were led to believe in 1990s. Pak is no longer in position to sustain the movement openly with the supply of arms, ammunition and personnel. As a frontline partner of US led war against Terrorism, it can not easily play double role, suppressing terrorism at home and exporting it to India. People of J&K have participated in elections despite bycot call by the separatists and people have installed a government of their own choice. Though degree of voters participation is no measure of pro-India feelings in the valley, but it undermines the belief that problem of governance, development and civic issues can not be postponed till Kashmir issue is finally resolved. To that extent the appeal of militancy has lost its urgency. Disillusionment with the armed movement across LOC is no less pronounced. Sadar Qayum Khan is senior leader of Azad Kashmir held that the worst damage to the Kashmir issue has been caused by the Jehadis who have no future, it is all over. It is of course no point for complicancy on part of Indian government that militancy has ended, but certainly it indicates that militancy in J&K has started losing its popular support.

Pak also feels that it has reached proportionately very close to Indian military strength. But it fails to recognise that the military power primarily rests upon industrial might and the power determines the strategic importance of the country. Since its inception Pak persuemed that against India, offence would have more advantage. Hence it has spent more on military capabilities and has number times invaded India. Pak has also acquired nuclear capabilities with a view to gain dominance and some sort of strategic importance in the region.

As regards Kashmir issue, there are people in Pak who have built empires and immense clout, their fear will vanish if reconciliation was reached. They want to use it as a bogey to keep people of Pak a hotage to their vested interests.

One of the Pak critics attributed the better relationship between the two countries as follows:-

"Pak was neither an aberration of history, nor a by product of British conspiracy, as perceived and brushed aside by pseudo secularists. It is based on solid foundations of its people, who wanted to have a separate homeland, and was created out of mutual agreement of the epoch-making historical forces that decided the fate of the sub-continent in its struggle for self determination. Unfortunately the Indian notion that Pak will not survive and Nehru's nationalism that adopted and extended Monroe Doctrine to India's small neighbours reinforced the paranoia of fear stricken state of Pak India's hegemonic expressions and hostility also fecilitated Pak seek its identity in ante Indian nations and ideological justification and support from elsewhere to counter balance an adversary. The dialectic led into motion mutually reinforcing Chauvinist and aggressive ideologies that have kept relationship between the two independent nations a hostage to adversity. Consequently, the differences were turned into conflicts and wars were fought to perpetuate disputes. Even if efforts were made to resolve them through negotiation. They were not meant to build a sound edifice of friendship on whose strength such intractable disputes as Kashmir could be resolved."

The view point of Pak critic are well taken. This may be one of the many reasons, which are apparent today in instigating hatered between the two countries. There may be some ideological difference in the thinking and policies of the two neighbours, but it does not permit anyone of them to resort to covert means like sponsering terrorism and get peace loving and innocent people killed for no fault of theirs. In a civilized society, the difference between the two nations are always sorted out at the diplomatic level. The ordent desire of the common people of India and Pak for peace and normal good relations between the two neighbouring countries has not been in doubt. There have been three wars between the two countries which have led to economic crisis which effects common people. There has been no ever lasting peace, as the outcome of these wars. Now to contemplate something as horrible as a nuclear confrontation is something which both countries and their people would turn their back on. The time is ripe that both realized the futility of negative and regid attitudes and sat down to resolve all outstanding issues with a somewhat flexible approach.

There are a number of major outstanding issue like Kashmir, demilitarization of Siachen and Sir Creec. There are big hurdles in solving these issues like the approach to Kashmir problem are at tangent by the two countries and hence a longtime stalemate. As regards demilitarisation of the world's highest battlefield is concerned, Indians do not trust Pak in that they feel soon it is vocated the Pak troops will once again occupy these heights of Siachen. Siachen is strategic for India because it overlooks the Karakoram Pass that links Pak to Aksai chin, part of erstwhile J&K state illegally ceded by Pak to China. Hence incase of hostilities between the two where China becomes an active partner, its land army has to cross over only through this pass. The controller of this pass can conveniently interfere with such movements.

The recent developments of Indo-Pak relations is viewed by political analysits as a march towards goodwill initiation. As delegations of peace, political leaders, people from media have been allowed to exchange their views is a happy situation in the offing. What is required to make upcoming composite dialogues achieveable is let bygones be by gone approach. It is high time for action not words as people of both the sides are politically conscious. Of course it is of utmost importance that Pak stops carrying out terrorist attacks time and again in India, killing large number of innocent people, which will certainly pose serious hinderence in peace process. The bomb blast in Samjhauta Express in February 2007 is one of the many torrorists actions which aim at distablizing Indian and derail the peace process about which one is even not very sure, if Pak is really willing for or it is a cover plan for the fundamentalist to go on unabated.

Although the only occasions when India and Pak have come close to peace have been during the brief periods of democratic rule in Pak. India has played no less role in helping General Musharaff gain legitimacy from the time it invited him out of the blue to the 2001 Agra summit, an invitation which helped lift the dictator's semi pariah status internationally. Today, as Mr Bush props up Musharaff's rule with multibillion dollar's aid and arms transfers India not only refrains from speaking about democrary in Pak but also in a major policy reversal, has come to accept Pak as a fellow victim of and partner against terrorism. By publically decoupling Pak from terrorism India has initiated a joint counter-terror mechanism. With what it had called a terrorist sponser until recently. It is no small irony that even India has become a pardonee - cum- partner. Presently it is only US that periodically shed new lights on Pak continued nexus with terrorism. Though General Musharaff sings the song which pleases Mr Bush, who has been lulled to believe that this military ruler remains a trusted ally.

India has to be very careful with the changed stance of Pak leadership who are voluntarily initiating peace talks yet their fundamentalists and Jehadis go on unabated with their terrorist attacks on Indian people. How come a mastermind of Kargil and the IC-814 hijacking has of late been singing a more conciliatry line on India even while shining the spotlight on Kashmir. Such political stagecraft, at a time when his main priority is to engineer his re election, keeps India fixated on his good relations bait, which presents him in the world eyes as a good peace maker. It matters very little that his Kashmir proposals, repeated in one from or the other since 2004, are based on the ideas conceived by New York based Kashmir Study Group, who depend largely on inputs from US.

Conclusion

What Pak has failed to appreciate or has deliberately closed its eyes to, is that nation power is a function of maternal assets and industrial and economic advancement. Pak in relation to India is way down in scale in all economic, technical and industrial capabilities. Pak persuemed that against India offensive doctrine will work better, but has miserably failed in all her attempts. Now she has resorted to sponsering terrorism in India, least realizing that such campaigns are short lived and very rarely succeeded even against relatively weak nations. Pak also does not realize that such operations once fail, back fire very badly; it strikes hard on its sponsers. Since its inception as independent state, Pak has harboured some false and ill conceived perceptions against India, which to a large extent blocked development of friendly relations with India, rather thus has become part of Pak Psyche. Instead of realizing the futility of conflict with India, Pak feels that through calandestive lows intensity subversive activities it can bleed the Indian nation and inflect heavy damage to its national power.

Some of the major factors which affect the relations are

(a) Pak feels that India never wanted to lose Pak to be an independent State and the government of India also holds the same view. Pak indentified India as the enemy No 1 and seeks parity in all spheres including armed forces, thereby badly losing on its economic growth.

(b) Pak does not accept J&K as legal part of India and is out to snatch it away at whatever be the cost. It is now busy sponsering terrorism from across the border to help dissidents in Kashmir to revolt.

(c) Pak from the beginning was created as a muslim state whereas India is a secular country where muslims have full right at par with Hindus. India is a democratic country where all decisions are taken by the elected representatives of the people. In Pak more often it is military rule, that too as the present, one can not operate at will when it comes to dealing with the aspects relating to religion. They are often influenced by ISI while making policies on Kashmir or helping US in war on terrorism.

(d) In a military rule like Pak, key decisions are made by a small coterie, without wider consultations and such decisions often prove retrograde.

(e) The acquisition of nuclear weapons by Pak add a new chapter to the threat perception from a

> military ruled state, where solutions to all problems in military language lie in the use of force. What Pak fails to understand that with acquisition of nuclear weapons, it has drawn itself close to mutual assured destruction. If war comes, it would be sheer madness for anyone to think of using these weapons, particularly Pak because of its geogrphical handicap and the socio-political constrants.

The nub of India-Pak rivalry remains irreconcilable-differences over their respective regional power aspirations and intimately related nuclear issues. Pak sees acquisition of nuclear weapons as a kind of equalizer, even if it could never hope to match India weapon for weapon.

The Kashmir issue remains a flesh point for bitter relations of two countries. If the Kashmir problem could somehow be settled with satisfaction to both the countries, the result would be significant. But the ideological conflict will persist as long there are mutual fears and people to exploit them. Kashmir crystallises the fear, the mistrust and the begotry that darken the sub continent and provides a vehicle for enlarging them with modern political complications. The confrontation of Islam and Hinduism is an echo of the religious wars.

It is notable that nearly sixty years of independence have produced no fundamental changes in the outlook of the two countries towards each other. On the contrary leaders on both sides react to crisis like their predecessors did in the past. Pak continues to believe without any solid evidence that India poses a prepetual threat to its national security. The religious prejudices and national apprehensions would have definitely reduced if there were no planned propagandas.

The Kashmir issue is delibrately kept alive and has been frequently exaggreated by Pak. It is of only secondary military significance in the Indo-Pak confrontation since military threat to each nation is across plains of Punjab and not the mountain ravines of Kashmir. In Pak, to keep the issue of Kashmir burning, is a strong point for sustenance of any leader, civilian or in military uniform.

It can be argued that Kashmir as an Indo-Pak issue has been insoluble since 1948. At that time it was clear that the tribal invasions had transformed the state into a symbol of military face for the uncertain new nations that neither would voluntarily withdraw from the captured areas during combat and there would be no bargaining. Therefore the resultant legalism and point of plibicite may have been well meant but were unrealistic. As the situation stablized after 1948 Kashmir operations, Pak's arguement for 1949 settlement lost validity and it became irrelevant subsequently.

Kashmir has become such an issue for the countries that their foreign policies are affected and politics is piosoned. Today neither of the countries seriously threatens each other security and stability with the armament in hand including nuclear arsenal. Military leaders in Pak though feel that they can topple Indian government by sponsering terrorism which has badly failed in every aspect. India has ever been ready for a dialogue with Pak, but Pak leaders do not seem comfortable at home when they talk of it, due to constant fundamentalists and ISI pressure. ISI is trying to raise a cry of Jehad against India and General Musharaff describes Jehad as the religious duty of every muslim. It appears that ISI has grown well tall, working in tandom with the terrorist groups and rebels in Northern provinces of Pak and it may not be very unfair to imagine ISI getting totally out of control of the military regime of Pak itself.

Pak also must realize that peace with India will not only release these resources presently tied in maintaining adverse relations with India, for more productive use and social uplift. It will yield additional economic developments by opening up mutually beneficial trade and commerce betwen the two countries. In short it is Pak, who would gain much more than India by improving relations.

Though of late, the two countries have taken some steps to improve relations between them; setting up bus service between Srinagar and Muzzarabad, this would help Kashmiris on both sides of the LOC to meet their relatives, other proposal include a rail link between Munabao (Rajasthan) - Khokrapar (Pak) and a ferry service between Mumbai and Karachi. Both the sides are also trying to improve sports ties and simplifying visa facilities. In order to ensure that the moves are useful and result oriented, the leadership on both the sides have to be sincere in their approach rather than a rhetoric for domestic consumption.

As regards trade between two countries since 1989, it has been negligible, when dispute over the rate of exchange between the two led to a total cessation of commercial relationship. Indo-Pak relations have matured as on date on the infrastructure of historical mistrust and unresolved territorial dispute and communal tension. These factors are a big hurdle in reaching normalcy in relations between these two neighbours.

Pak was carved out as a homeland for muslims, so its islamalization was inevitable. What is inexcusable is the radicalisation of Pak society under military rulers, who reared the Jehadi monster for narco-terrorism. General Musharaff is trying to show a soft approach towards Kashmir issue and the people feel with that there is decline in cross border terrorism. Infact it is not so. The Pak sponsored terrorists are now striking across the length and breadth of India. India is today fighting Pak's proxy war on multiple fronts. India should not get carried away by what General Musharaff says. They should weigh all pros and cons of the peace proposals. How can a right thinking person digest that on one hand peace talks are scheduled to take place in Delhi between the two governments and a day prior, there are serial bomb blasts in Samjhauta Express killing innocent people, belonging to both the countries. This shows either the military ruler have lost control over their ISI and Jehadis or they are not well meaning in there dealings. It would therefore be totally unwise for Indian government to put all its eggs in General Musharaff's basket. It should buy itself some insurance by forging links with the democratic parties of Pak as well. After the proposed elections in late 2007, should martial law be reimposed and democratic movement develop in opposition to it, India should then seize the opportunity to render all possible help to them even at international forum, rather than maintaining a studied neutrality. If Pak returns to democracy, the historical records show that no two democracies have ever gone for war against each other. This is because democracies routinely use non-violent ways to resolve diferences. It is only the prorogative of the military rulers to use military force, to all the problems as an universal solution.

The next question is how to deal with Pak sponsered terrorism in J&K and the country as a whole. Following are few ways to get over this menace.

(a) Continue Peace dialogues with Pak leadership, a good sense may prevail over them and may realize the futility of such action at such a cost.

(b) Ignore Pak actions as only of a nuisance value, but this is not easy since constant pin pricks by a weaker adversary may result in serious wounds for a strong nation like India, incase of delayed reaction to curb this nuesance.

(c) The other alternative is to expose Pak to the world community as a state sponsering and abetting terrorism. Though result of such diplomatic overtures are self interest based and are very slow in showing up.

16

MILITARY RULE IN PAK AND ITS LIKELY FUTURE

There is no dearth of politicians, thinkers and strategists in Pak who claim that the country was the result of a democratic process and Mr Jinnah was a great democrat. But there were certain mistakes made by Mr Jinnah which made the Pak army brass taste the power. His orders to the army to capture Kashmir came at a time when political leadership in the country was not settled yet. The British trained army and bureaucracy had a natural antipathy towards the politicians. Thus the 1947-48 Kashmir war gave army a chance to organise and strengthen itself at a time when Mr Jinnah himself was not clear as to what system of government would suit Pak. Kashmir being a muslim majority area became a test case for the two nation theory or the ideology of Pak. The army felt that the armed forces in Pak are not only meant to guard the geographical boundaries but also the ideological frontiers of Pak. In other words, the test of two nations theory on Kashmir provided the army a justification to be involved in the affairs of the state so to counter anti-ideology forces. As was seen during General Zia ul Haq that the army was totally involved in all the affairs of the state and he used the name of ideology and Islam to remove democracy from Pak.

After Mr. Jinnah's death, the army in Pak started making way for its eventual capture of power right from January 1951, when General Ayub Khan took over as C-in-C Pak army. There started assassination of political leaders so to clear the way for the army to establish its domain. On 16 october 1951 Mr Liaquat Ali the Prime Minister of Pak was killed in Rawalpindi under mysterious circumstances. It was seen as a move to nip democracy in the bud. There were some other important politicians who met similar fate for opposing military dictatorship in the country. Elimination of Mr Z A Bhutto, a very popular leader, by a military ruler on flimsy grounds was yet another move to keep democracy at bay. But whatever Mr Jinnah had in mind about the system of government in Pak, it was not the military system, though he had defaulted by ordering military action in Kashmir at a time when the political leadership in Pak was in a fluid state and he was too old and sick to exert.

The Constitution which was promulgated on 23 March 1956 could only survive for about nine years, until the martial law imposed by President Iskandar Mirza.

There was no constitution in the country between 1958 to 1962. General Ayub Khan drafted another constitution for the country in 1962 to meet his requirement, which abolished the party system.

He designed the constitution to ensure his survival, but when he failed he handed over the reign to the next military ruler, General Yahya Khan in March 1969. General Yahya Khan conducted the general elections in 1970, but seeing the results going against his assessment, amended the constitution to give him five years as the President of Pak.

In 1973, the constitution was again evolved, supposedly with the concensus of the political parties of Pak. This was again suspended during the Civil Disobedience Movement under the plea that there was no need to strike a balance between the powers of President and Prime Minister. The aim was to make the presential system of government where President would be all powerful even to appoint or dismiss the PM and ministers. General Zia advocated that the Presidential form of government was the most suited to countries like Pak and that even Mr Jinnah favoured this type of system of governance.

The army's addiction to power has rendered the Pak constitution making an absolutely sterile activity. In its quest for power, the army observes no rules and cares about no consequences. But what is strange is that all military rulers are able to convince their masses in

Pak against democracy and public too likes strong and ruthless handling.

Pak has been hit by number of martial laws. The martial law carries with it the cancerous legacies of the previous regimes under military rule. In addition it develops its own gangrane. Though over the period people have realized that martial law is devoid of the attributes to dispence law. Ayub Khan and Yahya Khan were honest enough to admit that marital law was an expedient and not a law. The sanction of force stands behind the medley of personal order and regulations of martial law. The sanction of the people's consent stands behind the heirarchy of the laws. In one situation the population is regimented into acquiescence. In the other the population voluntarily establishes a contract with Parliament. In one situation the relationship is based on how far the bayonet reaches from the centre of power to the centre of population. In the other word how far the voice travels between the governing and the governed. For this reason one is called regime and other government. Martial law rests on the sanction of force and not on the sanction of law.

It is true that Pak was created in the name of Islam. But these were the masses of Pak who did it under civilian leadership and not under the military generals. So let the people decide as to how to run this country. Besides, Islam does not exist in Pak alone it is all over the world. Saudi Arabia which is the spiritual centre of Islam has been marching ahead without Pak like dramatics, under the leadership of Saudi Royal family.

Civilization means civil supremacy. Continued military rule is a disaster. Infact strictly speaking the only Coup d'etat that brought glory to its people was that of Napolean Bonaparte. He was a giant. He was an outstanding leader. His military brilliancy was only one facet of his many sided genius. His Napoleonic code remains the basic law of many countries. He was an excellent administrator and a scholar. Even this military dictator with his undoubted genius, took France to agony of Waterloo.

The cover plan to overthrow all civilian government by martial law in Pak has been nicknamed as 'civil war'. There have also been a large number of attempted coups in Pak since independence. In 1951, the government of Liaquat Ali Khan suppressed the attempted Coup d'etat of Major General Mohd. Akbar Khan, Chief of General Staff of Pak army. PM, Liaquat Ali Khan condemned the attempted military take over in the strongest of terms. He called the conspirators the enemies of democracy. He warned the generals to keep away from politics for the welfare of Pak and its unity. He described the coup leader as selfish individual. The coup d'etat was crushed and civil war did not follow. On the other hand had the conspirators succeeded they would have called themselves a saviour of Pak. Towards the end of 1972 and the beginning of 1973 barely a year after a traumatic civil war had ended with separation of Bangladesh, another coup by comparatively junior officers, who were related to various politicians was prematurely detected and suppressed.

Certainly armies are called to suppress rebellions, insurgencies and revolts, but a temporary contengency should not be converted into permanent feature of national life. A separate and parallel authority can not be created above the supreme and sovereign Parliament on a flimsy pretext. Two sovereign can not co-exist under one sovereignty. Such a situation provides no place for politics and if there is no place for politics, that there is no place left for polity.

In one system the ascendancy is of civil elected government and in the other is the ascendancy of the political party. In both the cases the army is subordinate to the central government. If the sovereignty of the country is not safe in the hands of its elected representatives, it can be safe in no other hands.

The policy of all martial law regimes has been as part of an attempt at self prepetuation at the cost of unity and integrity of the country to induct army officers into the civil services so to make civil mechinary totally ineffective and under control. This policy is persued with a vengeance by the military regimes. This sets in sense of demoralization and insecurity among civil servants especially because a regular flow of all level army officers coming to civil administration and blocking their promotional avenues. Power has its own taste and in course of time particularly the middle rung military officers, start relishing the power in form of arrest, searches and interrogations of civil public, which gives them feel of authority. They also develop contempt for the ways of politicians and civil servants and a general impression in the army circle is that everybody in the field of civil administration and politics are incompetent and corrupt and only army can deliver goods.

Army therefore should not be frequently involved in civil administration except in emergencies in aid to civil authorities that too for a limited time. It should not become a law enforcing agency. Prolonged role of army in dealing with internal situation has its limitations and its mission becomes self prepetuating.

Throughout the political history of Pak, two factors have emerged conspicuously; one, the army rule and two the religion. The intact fuedal structure and religious institutions all work in tandem for the common aim of retaining the power. This poses serious threat to social and democratic transformation of the society and the country. Everyone in power, irrespective of type of rule, exploited masses in the name of Islam. This process of using name of religion worked to the advantage of previlleged segment of society namely military, bureaucracy, landlords and the industrialists. The military rulers find use of religion as a great help in continuing in power by misleading the common masses.

Since Pak's independence only the small previlleged minority, feudal aristocracy, strengthened by the induction of retired military officers and civil bureaucrats reaped the benefits of economic gains in terms of better training, education economic prosperity and political participation. The economic gains hardly reach the deprived masses of Pak.

Pak also started as democratic state which envisaged advancement of people and progress of the country. It was planned to use instrument of a liberal Parliamentary system to achieve the desired goals, however it remains short lived.

Almost after two years of independence, aberrant and Freakish turn and twists of national politics ended with real power resting in the hands of military rulers. Political powers and authorities were no longer in the hands of politicians, it was snatched away time and again by the military generals. This happened not because there was a political vaccume, since there were large number of competent people in the field. This happened because military leaders were supported by bureaucrats in siezure of political power.

In Pak Constitutional history, neither the politicians nor military leaders respected the basic law. The review of political development reveals that egalitarian power structure which the country inherited from the colonial era; remained intact with power concentration in military and bureaucracy with backing from feudal class.

The power group are not keen in establishing democratic norms as it eroded their power and previlleges. The urban middle class, independent professionals and intelligentsia, who have interest in promoting democracy, have become somewhat politically marginalized.

Since independence, Pak completed for the first time in May 1977, the longest period (over ten years) of Parliamentary democracy without interruptions. The absolute power has corrupted the Pak rulers. Though corruption is not only confined to Pak, but in other countries it is abhorred and severely criticized and punished, whereas in Pak, because of absolute power in the hands of military rulers, it flourishes with impunity.

General Zia utilized the process of Islamisation to achieve his political ends and sought legitimacy by implementing islam as an ideology of Pak. He with the help of State institutions, weakened the secular and progressive forces of the country. He introduced Federal Shariat courts which proved law demolishing agency in conflict with Parliament as the constitutionally sovereign legislative body. The islamisation which has been used as a political weapon time and again, has caused severe damage to Pak national life. Wrong interpretation of Islam has resulted in the rise of fundamentalism, obscurantism and retrogression. Women became the special victims of Islamisation of law and its inconsistancies.

Islam which should have served to unite the people of Pak is being misused to divide them into mutually hostile sectarian groups and to divert their attention from basic social and economic problems.

The military rulers are responsible for supression and distortion of political process as far as loss of sense of belonging, which is very essential for the survival of a country. They divide the community into 'Biradaries' and tribes. The governance has been reduced merely to the previlleged, delinking power from responsibility and confusing opportunism with leadership.

The people of Pak have tried hard to opt for Parliamentary democracy since independence. There have been many changes in the government ranging from democracy to dictatorship. The people of Pak have been mute spectators to the events of dismissal of elected governments and abrogation of the constitution. This has been because of tug of war for power between the Army and the politicians to retain power and control the government in Pak. Politicians in Pak have always blamed the military for its extra constitutional role in politics. On the other hand the military has blamed politicians for their misgovernance and corruption, justifying military rule as the only way to irradicate these menace from the society.

There have also been confrontation between Prime Minister and President over the control of the government. The constitution of the country was amended many times, sometimes by the PM and the other time by the President in order to shift power to self. General Zia by the 8th amendment to the constitution of 1973 made himself supreme but Mr Nawaz Shariff discarded the amendment when he became PM and by the 13th amendment he divested the President of powers to dismiss the PM. But soon after General Pervez Musharaff took over the reigns of Pak, he again amended the constitution and restored the powers of the President to dismiss the PM.

Mr. Jinnah had always envisioned a democratic Pak and many of his successors have tried towards this goal, but their self interest and greed for power has always been above everything, even the interest of the country. Pak today faces the unenviable task of setting government priorities in accordance with the needs of the people today. There are some well to do families with rich heritage, who have been mastering not only the politics but the trade, Industry, Banking, Administration, Police and Military since independence of Pak. Democracy thus got stuck at the alter of family politics and governance based on self interest. The political parties have handled the people as herds of sheep, not letting them actively participate in the nation building. This is the fundamental cause which has kept Pak deprived of democratic culture. Constitution was made but its sanctity was never respected. Politicians and army both are busy looking for opportunity to snatch power from each other at the first occasion. When a country is governed disregarding the natural principles of justice and rationality, the result is – repeated mistakes, leading the country to Chaos. Pak today is once again at the cross roads looking for a permanent alternative for itself, for its people who need equality and fundamental rights under the constitution.

Pak return to democracy rests on a few complex factors some of which are internal and some external. Internally Mr Nawaj Shariff and Ms Benazir Bhutto have to work unitedly and carryout programme to mobalize masses against the military rule in Pak. For this most important would be, as seen in the history of Pak, particularly in the case of late Mr Z A Bhutto, to harness Pak students power for democratic movement. The support of parties like MMA and other would be useful. Externally it is US who has to feel that General Musharaff is not indespensable for the US strategic interests. The stability of Pak lies in permanent democracy and not in make shift military rules. The stability of Pak would have positive bearing on overall well being of South Asia. It looks, US is not much interested about the type of government in Pak but it only worries of the transfer of power in the hands of fundamentalists, Islam radicals which is the worst case for them and the world. As long General Musharaff toes US line, they are happy.

India should also not show its weakness by agreeing to temporary peace proposal by the military regime of Pak. The world, particularly the US should not allow Pak to continue as a dictatorship with all its propensity for military misadventure from Al Qaeda to Taliban and Islamic Jehad in Kashmir. Democracy must return to Pak in the interest of its people and the muslim world. What we see today in Pak is concentration of power at the centre by the military rulers, which is generally unresponsive to the basic needs of people and riding rough shod over the interests and aspirations of people of Pak.

The empowerment of people, of course has to be integral part of the overall project of strengthening the civil society in a true democracy. The democratically organised political parties, independent and free press and also the electronic media workers and peasants groups are the pre requisites of the civil society. 'People should feel free to discuss and decide issues that concern their lives such as work, health, education, housing, environment, gender equality and human rights etc. First and foremost the people of Pak will have to put up a bold and concrete plan into effect to dismantle the highly centralized unitary and authoritarian structure of Pak. Democracy in any form can not co-exist with a state in which power is centralized and which is throughly alienated from the civil society.

It is totally wrong to preach or believe that democracy failed in Pak in 1950 and again during Bhutto's rule. Democracy should be allowed a continuous run at least for 15 years to know if it fails or succeeds, because it is only then that people will become politically aware and national unity will be forged. The military can not claim that its rule has been successful. Infact it is otherway.

The Likely Future of Military Rule in Pak

General Musharaff told his countrymen that next elections would be held by the end of 2007 and the dates will be decided by the Election Commission of Pak. He also confirmed that there was no bar for a condidate to become President for as many times. He emphasized very categorically that no country could force another one that its President could not be the Chief of Army in addition to being the President of that country. Making the case for his continuation as the Army Chief and President, General Musharaff said by virtue of holding the two posts he was able to maintain the unity of command, allowing him to take important decisions relating to national security. General Musharaff further clarified that two-third majority in Parliament allowed him to keep the two posts and that it was according to democratic procedure of the country. Though the general promised free and fair election after November 2007 in the country, but said that leaders living outside Pak will not be allowed to return, but their parties can take part in Parliamentary polls. This way he planned to ward off real threat of losing power to Mr Nawaz Shariff and Ms Benazir Bhutto's popular political parties.

There appears no chance of democracy returning to Pak in near future, particularly after separation of Bangladesh which could exert some kind of pressure on the army while it was part of Pak. The public particularly Punjab seems to have got used to army rule. Even certain elites, surprisingly are not attracted towards democracy because they experienced repression and authoritarianism during Mr Z A Bhutto's government. The army in Pak will always play a card of threat from India to keep themselves in power. Being a feudal society, divided in different creeds, castes and clans, the people of Pak are not too keen for democracy. They easily get worked up in the name of religion, which sentiment is exploited by the army ruler particularly when it comes to dealing with India. But for Pak's survival, democracy is a must. The political leaders must change their attitude towards Islam. Right from day one of Pak movement, Islam has been used as a negative force. This still persists. If Pak breaks up again, it will not be because of people or politicians of Pak but because of its military rulers.

Pak is most interesting country, where army generals play open game of politics and in the process they become tools in the hands of super power. Military leaders do not hold elections unless they have to. The martial law will continue to be imposed when needed by the army. This happens because of taste of power by the military heirarchy, for generals top slots and for the junior rung officers, administration job are reserved.

This way a professional army damages itself, apart from damaging the political system since they are not meant for running the country's government. Newly independent States, when they lose patience with untidy and slow moving democratic process, turn to temptation of authoritarian rule, only to discover later that they have made a serious damage to their country, particularly so because this becomes a habit for the military rulers to acquire political power at will.

The long rule of General Musharaff has proved that war against terror and political extremism can not be fought through military means alone. The replacement of institution by a military ruler thwarts the growth of civil society, besides being distablizing for the polity General Musharaff has prevented mainstream liberal parties from functioning freely so to ensure that these parties did not uproot him in the coming elections, if at all these were held.

For a period the General Musharaff has been in power, Pak internal situation and international image have gone down in the ratings. Military rule which was justified to erradicate corruption and bring stability to the country has driven the country to the wall; internationally Pak is viewed a frontline state breeding terrorism.

General Musharaff who went from asserting 'Jehad is an instrument of Pak Policy', to professing to promote enlightened moderation post 9/11, has given rise to extremism and terrorism. Now he is busy planning to stay in power for atleast next five more years, beyond 2007. He plans to get the outgoing Parliament and four provincial legislatures to elect him beforehand to a new five year term as President and then oversee the national polls a little later. Though the coming general elections are not likely to be free and fair as were in 2002. But by the above plan he wants to play very safe. His sinking popularity has spurred speculations that he, not content with his current authorititarian rule, might declare a state of emergency. Since General Musharaff is losing his popularity, he is becoming more dependent on his army and the intelligence system, which inhabit his move to sever their ties with the extremists and terrorists. His main benefactor, the US President has got totally involved in war with Iraq that he has no time to read the game General Musharaff has been playing, including openly helping Taliban against NATO forces in Afganistan.

In the overall analysis, it is assessed that military rule under General Pervez Musharaff is likely to continue at least for the next five years, since there is no worthwhile political leader who could challenge his authority. He has already declared that Mr Nawaz Shariff and Ms Benazir Bhutto will not be allowed to take part in the coming general elections. This coupled with US, unconditional support to his military regime, the general has no fears of anykind except spordic terrorist attacks, which are also the part of his own doings.

The above assessment is based on the premise that General Musharaff continues to enjoy the trust of Mr Bush, despite the fact that Pak under General Musharaff is playing double game. Should this game plan unfold and US, particularly Mr Bush realizes his mistake of blindly trusting General Musharaff who is not at all sincere to him, the General may be shown the exit and some, replacement from the Pak army itself may be found for him. This though appears a remote possibility, unless the events turn faster than expected.

Unlike the previous military rulers Ayub and Zia, who had solid support of a more homogenous ruling class, Musharaff lacks that and has no constituency or support base. The religious fundamentalists are not happy with him. The only support comes to him is from US, which is also need based. Any strict military like behaviour is likely to back fire, like it happened in March 2007 when General Musharaff dismissed Chief Justice of Pak Supreme Court Mr Chaudhary on very flimsy grounds and the public and the Pak intellectual came to the streets against his decision. The general had no choice than to retrieve to save his chair. Even some of the senior army officers showed anger on this decision of General Musharaff; because everyone knew the motive to dismiss Mr Chaudhary, a strict judge, was to get rid of him before the elections in November 2007.

Pak's economy is also in deep trouble. Obviously a major drain on the country's economic resources is heavy expenditure on defence, combined now with added cost of nuclear technology and weapons. This of course is done to maintain adverserial relations with India, which serves no worthwhile purpose, except pleasing the illitrate masses of the country.

Pak's education system is abysmal by all standards. While the rich can afford to send their children to good convent schools and also abroad, but the education system for the public is very poor. The poor education system is directly contributing to the popularity of fundamentalists ideologies and support for the militancy. The public who can not afford high cost of education, perforce have to send their children to Madarsas, which are more of religious institutions, meant to indoctrionate young boys towards Jehad. These madarsas are serving as a nursery for the militants.

Pak is depicted a nation of contridictions replete with pockets of thriving guns and drug culture and prone to act of terrorism. It is now to be seen if General Musharaff can steer Pak on the right track and prevent impending Chaos. Pak is a nation which is lodged between a weak democracy and benevolent autocracy since its inception. A good portion of feudal aristocracy has accepted the role of a second string to the military supremacy.

If democracy has to come to Pak, the powers have to be decentralized. It can not co-exist in any form in which all the powers are centralized and which is throughly alienated from the civilian society. The concentation of power in the centre results in frequent dismissal of elected government and to solve all the problems, they apply coercive force rather than political negotiations with disasterous social and political consequences. The empowerment of people has to be an integral part of the overall project of strengthening the civil society.

Pak does not need military rule to deal with terrorists or for catching Al Qaeda fugitives. Return to democracy can help Pak to avoid a situation where militants determine and decide a course for Pak's destiny.

General Musharaff extended his Presidency for five years by a referendum. It is now for the people of Pak to judge what referendum means in terms of returning the country to democratic civilian rule. It is also felt that as long as General Musharaff's regime allows US and allied troops to use its territory in dealing with Taliban, Pak's internal politics and its own interests will remain secondary and neglected.

General Musharaff has shown willingness to hold elections for Parliament in November 2007, but he will not risk civilian scrutiny until it can guaruntee the continuation of his own entrenched power in the Pak society.

Mr Stephen Phillip Cohen writes in his book 'The Idea of Pakistan' on the options available to US with regard to Pak.

"America must remember that although Pak will pursue its own vital interests as it sees them, an opportunity may exist to shape Pak's future in a direction that is compatible with American (and Pak) interests. Pak has demonstrated an ability to resist America in the case of its nuclear programme, its provocative policy on Kashmir, its tolerance of domestic extremism and its support for the Taliban. In each case, Washington was unable to persuade Pak that these policies threatened vital Pak interests, as well American ones. Before writing Pak off as a hopelessly failed state, that its critics believe it to be, Washington may have one last opportunity to ensure that this troubled State will not become America's biggest foreign policy problem in the last half of the decade".

The suspension of Pak Supreme Court Chief Justice on 09 March 2007 by General Musharaff has astounded everyone. The political impropriety of the unconstitutional action is apparent since Mr Chaudhary is an honest and law abiding citizen, which does not suit General Musharaff's plans for future and his apprehensive pre election martial impulse. The procedure followed by the military ruler in suspending the Chief Justice was contrary to the provisions of article 209 of Pak's constitution, which can not be tinkered by capricious executive action. There were public agitations against this action and the military government was heavy handed and used excessive force to quell dissent. This military crackdown on Pak judiciary and press were shown all over on TV and internet, inviting wide spread condemnation from the civil society and press, world over. Though US only advised both the sides in Pak to exercise restraint and further supported Musharaff saying that he is pro-democracy patriot who is acting in the best interest of Pak. With decade of good deal with Pak military than civil society, US is in no mood to disinvest in countrys security driven establishment.

The Judiciary in Pak is also to be blamed to some extent for such treatment, since they have been tolerating such action on part of the military rulers in the past, without any noise. In 1977 the Pak Supreme Court ruled in Begum Nusrat Bhutto Vs Chief of Army Staff, Pak army, that the Chief Martial Law Administrator, General Zia ul Haq, had validly assumed power by means of an extra constitutional step, in the interest of the State and for the welfare of the people. It was infact this authoritative pronouncement made thirty years ago, that gave courage to successive regimes to deface the constitution. A judiciary that has itself in past lagitimised extra constitutional step, should not now crib, having set the precedence themselves.

General Musharaff has given a fenciful account of himself and his role in the Kargil conflict with India in 1999 in his book 'In the line of Fire'. The book also gives out his other achievements in Pak during his tenure, just to project his image in public. But what is seen on ground is only believed by the public, therefore he should talk less and what he says should be converted into action if he is really serious to refurbish his reputation. A military ruler making lose statement, only for public consumption, is seen by the elite group as his bankurpcy in diplomacy.

The future of Pak lies in the tussle between the moderates and the extremists. General Musharaff once said that he was keen to create a moderate country which was in the interest of all and as such essential to dispel the growing impression in the world of Pak being irresponsible and a rouge state. His number of actions towards liberalisation in Pak, though much to the dislikes of fundamentalists, are towards moderation.

Some of the internal developments in Pak also indicate that General Musharaff is gradually losing hold over his regime. The cases in point are the siding of retired generals openly with Mr Chaudhary, the suspended Chief Justice. This should not generally happen because the military ruler always takes full case of his predecessors, the retired military men. The other incident was where a group of female students occupied a public library in Islamabad to block General Musharaff's move to demolish two mosques that government claimed were iligally built. The government initially had to back off. But the problem has now been resolved. There was yet another incident when people from the troubled tribal areas joined hands with the lawyers and made the protest a complete success in shape of a strike. These are serious indication that political storm is brewing in Pak. There is also division in the army ranks, some are pro-US, whereas others do not relish General Musharaff helping US against Taliban. The general needs to aply discrect control over these incidents if he plans to remain President and army chief beyond October 2007. The general also should see in his own interest that these mullahs do not become too strong for him to handle. His latest actions to pass women protection bill and change in school carriculum which emphasized Jehad and martyrdom, have slightly toned down radicalism.

After the fall of Taliban in December 2001, Lashkar-e-Toiba and Jaise-e-Mohd shifted their camps from Afganistan to the Pak territory, but they continue to have links with Al Qaeda. These camps sometimes operate under the guise of madrasas or Koranic schools. It has been established that mujahideen from all over the world come for training to these camps and return to their areas for Jehad after completing there training. India has raised the issue of Pak sponsered terrorism time and again with Pak, but all in vain. These terrorist groups seem to have become too powerful for the military ruler to handle. Such display of weakness on part of Pak government will always provoke and encourage war where extremists would prevail. In fact most of the terrorist organisations have acknowledged their close connections with Al Qaeda. These organisations have immensely benifitted from Al Qaeda's monetary and technical resources.

The Bush administration is under pressure from its intelligence agencies to take punitive actions against Al Qaeda camps in Pak even though US publically continues to praise Musharaff as a stalwart ally in the war on terror. These agencies have given confirmed reports of Al Qaeda regrouping and rebuilding in Pak, but Bush under the circumstances is not paying much heed to these.

The fear within US that Islamic extremism has become dominant force in Pak, has been stoked in part by Musharaff himself. This though is taken by some analysts as a ploy by General Musharaff to maintain steady flow of US aid and also to keep US away from asking him for democratic reforms. Though there were some reports in media about US cutting of some aid to Pak and that they have started realizing that Musharaff is no more indispensable. But it seems very unlikely, particularly for Mr Bush that US will turn against his faithful ally. General Musharaff on his part also does not let the impression go totally negative and when required he moves against extremists and captures some to please the master. The capture of Mullah Obaidullah deputy of Taliban, from Quetta by Pak army was the action to keep the impatience of US under check. Though the capture was carried out reluctantly since it undermines Pak army's relations with Taliban. But is also true that Al Qaeda and other extremists are merely quarantined by Pak as state guests, when the heat is on and then set free when world attention shifts away.

Conclusion

In the overall analysis, it appears that the military rule in Pak has become a necessity under the present circumstances, to run the country. The army in Pak has played and continues to play a very vital role in shaping the destiny of the nation since independence. It is lodged between a weak democracy and benevolent autocracy since its inception. A good portion of feudal aristocracy has accepted the role of a second string to military supermacy since military in Pak has directly ruled the country for most of the time. In order to strengthen its hold on power, it has cultivated relations with the fundamentalists. The army has remained powerful even when they are not in power and as a rule they were always consulted before taking important decisions by the democratically elected government. Political leadership in Pak is always apprehensive of army's intervention on flimsy grounds since the army has enjoyed the taste of power.

The military rule in Pak has come to stay. Even if General Musharaff is forced to quit by US pressure because of political compulsions, he is most likely to be replaced by a militaryman. Even if civilian elected government comes in between, it is not likely to last for long due to prevailing Chaos in the country.

The political leadership in Pak is corrupt, chaotic, feudal and capitalist. They hardly bother for the welfare and uplift of the masses. The economic condition in the country is very poor and standard of education is very low. The weaker section of the society perforce have to send their children to madrasas run by the fundamentalists. One can imagine the future of such indoctrinated young generation of the country. The law and order in the country are non-existent. The extremists dictate terms to the government. The tribal areas which are semi-autonomous, already feel that they do not form part of Pak. This is particularly so because they are a neglected lot by the Punjabi dominated Pak government. Even the present military leadership, who have enormous powers, appears helpless in effectively governing Pak under the prevailing conditions. There appears no tall political leadership (non-tainted) in Pak today who can control the present chaos in the country even if they come to power. There are also apprehensions that if the elections are held without proper supervision, the fundamentalists may come to power and the existing nuclear arsenal in Pak, may pose a very serious and grave danger to world peace.

Democracy is a boon, bestowed upon the brave and courageous by the Almightty God. The people of Pak have to realize the importance of democracy, if they really want freedom for self and their generation. Today there appears no ray of hope of the militaryman disappearing from the political scene in Pak.

General Musharaff's popularity has been gradualy declining, particularly due to ongoing moves to sack the Chief Justice of Pak Supreme Court and clerics of Lal Masjid in Islamabad trying to impose Sharia law and want Talibanisation of Pak. General Musharaff's approach in dealing with the fundamentalists is seen as too soft. Lal Masjid controls two madrassas, Jamia Hafsa for girls and Jamia Farida for boys. There are approximately 6000 students in these madrasas who are mostly Pashtuns from NWFP, Talibanised and armed with weapons. In March 2007, these students, particularly burqa clad girls banned playing and selling musical CDs, and blew up a few shops with home made bombs, calling this business an unislamic. The radical clerics also issued a fatwa against Pak tourism minister, Nilofar Bakhtiar for hugging a male paratrooper during paragliding show in Paris. She feared for her life since the extremist elements had already killed a woman activist, Zille Huma, a provincial minister of Punjab. Though the problem of Lal Masjid has been carefully tackled by the military ruler for the present.

How General Musharaff addresses these problems, will affect the future of Pak. He is not likely to adopt hard approach against the clerics and these students of two madrassas since these students are Pashtuns and so is the majority of soldiers in Pak army. Voicing opposition to crackdown on radical islamic madrassas, which had demanded imposition of Shariah law, Pak rulling brass had argued that such a step would not be beneficial before the forth coming general elections and the situation in the provinces of Waziristan and Balochistan. Such a crackdown, they felt was likely to create a law and order problem and strengthen hands of extremists in Pak. What is scary about these events is that the epicentre of the new Talibanisation has shifted to the heart of the federal capital. The islamic vigilantism is likely to spread to the market places and shopping centres in Islamabad and other cities. The Kiosks selling pirated CDs and TV sets are likely to be the targets for attacks. Women not properly clothed and driving around in the cities are hooted on the roads.

Pak has become a nursary for islamic terrorism. Laskar-e-Toiba is reported to raise band of women militants of Kashmir origin and providing them ideological and arms training in the camps situated in POK. One of the primary tasks of these women would be to trap army officers and jawans to gain information. The special course called Daura-e-Sofa is given to women cadres drawn from madrassas in POK and the valley. Pak is now hit by a new wave of fundamentalism that can not be silenced by US funded arms. It could have been curbed by creating strong social and political processes that helped women get educated and children aspire for jobs. But what the military rules of Pak have done is to push civil society resistance to the mosque, where it has got radicalised.

General Musharaff is now trying to strike a deal with Benazir Bhutto of PPP (who is self exiled) for support to become President for the second term and also to form a common front against conservative religious forces in the country. It is reliably confirmed that the exiled former Prime Minister Ms Bhutto has agreed to support General Musharaff's reelection in return for the country's National Accountability Bureau dropping a host of corruption cases against her and her husband. The PPP would support General Musharaff's reeletion as President by the present assemblies which would be endorsed by the new houses after the general elections. However, it is reported that General Musharaff's continuation as army chief in addition, remained a bone of contention during the talks between emissaries of the two leaders in Dubai in March 2007.

The exiled PM, Mr Nawaz Shariff has also said that he would return to Pak at an appropriate time and that no one can stop him. The general is under growing international pressure to restore democracy in Pak. In view of his declining popularity and slight change in US attitudes towards his policies, it is speculated that General Musharaff might accept a Bhutto led government if it backs his Presidency and his changes to the constitution, which have given him sweeping powers and formalized the military's pervasive role in Pak politics.

In the ultimate analysis it is beyond doubt that whatever be the outcome of elections, the military elite in Pak will never disappear from the political scene of the country, at least in the foreseeable future.

BIBLIOGRAPHY

1. Friends Not Masters by F.M. Ayub Khan.

2. The Genocide in Bangladesh by Jag Mohan.

3. An End without beginning by Sayeed Ziaullah & Simuel Baid.

4. In Line of Fire by General Pervez Musharaff.

5. Sino-Pak Strategic Cooperation – Peace Initiatives.

6. If I am assassinated by Z.A. Bhutto.

7. The Indo-Pak Conflict by Russel Brines.

8. Twenty two Fateful days by D.R. Mankekar.

9. India answers Pakistan by B.G. Verghese.

10. The 17 days War by Major A.R. Siddiq – Pak Army.

11. Pakistan Crisis in Leadership by Major General F.M. Khan, Pak Army.

12. Government and Politics in Pakistan – Ahmed Mushtaq.

13. Generals in Politics : Pak – Mohd. Ashgar Khan.

14. Party Politics in Pak – K. K. Aziz.

15. The Great Tragedy – Z.A. Bhutto.

16. Pak: A Political Study – Callard Keith.

17. Indo-Pak Relations – Varindee Grover & Ranjan Arora.

18. Strategic Analysis – USI Journals.

19. India Today – Periodical.

20. News Paper – Times of India.

21. Slender Was the Thread – Lt. General L.P. Sen.

22. Pak's Foreign Policy – Shahid M. Amin.

23. The Idea of Pakistan – Stephen Phillip Cohen.